THE SIKH FAITH

A UNIVERSAL MESSAGE

GURBAKHSH SINGH

Sacha Sauda Gurmat Parchar Society
Brampton, ont, Canada
L6T 5T1

THE SIKH FAITH
(A Universal Message)
by
Gurbakhsh Singh

2007

Price   : 60/- Rs.

Published by : Sacha Sauda Gurmat Parchar Society
                   Brampton, ont, Canada
                   L6T 5T1

Laser Setting : Little Graphics, Jalandhar.

                                    Printed in India
Printed at   :   Artcave Printers, Ludhiana.

Dedicated
to
the Youth

On whose shoulders lie
the hope and responsibility of establishing
Truth, Justice and ever-lasting Peace
in the world.

INVOCATION

By the Grace of the Lord,
The Supremus, the Truth,
The Creator, Self-existent,
Vibrating in His creation,
Without apprehensions or hostility.
He alone was there before creation,
And He alone will ever be.

(Guru Granth, P. 1)

CONTENTS

ਤੂ ਠਾਕੁਰੁ ਤੁਮ ਪਹਿ ਅਰਦਾਸਿ ॥
ਜੀਉ ਪਿੰਡੁ ਸਭੁ ਤੇਰੀ ਰਾਸਿ ॥
ਤੁਮ ਮਾਤ ਪਿਤਾ ਹਮ ਬਾਰਿਕ ਤੇਰੇ ॥
ਤੁਮਰੀ ਕ੍ਰਿਪਾ ਮਹਿ ਸੂਖ ਘਨੇਰੇ ॥

ਕੋਇ ਨ ਜਾਨੈ ਤੁਮਰਾ ਅੰਤੁ ॥
ਊਚੇ ਤੇ ਊਚਾ ਭਗਵੰਤ ॥

ਸਗਲ ਸਮਗ੍ਰੀ ਤੁਮਰੈ ਸੂਤ੍ਰਿ ਧਾਰੀ ॥
ਤੁਮ ਤੇ ਹੋਇ ਸੁ ਆਗਿਆਕਾਰੀ ॥
ਤੁਮਰੀ ਗਤਿ ਮਿਤਿ ਤੁਮ ਹੀ ਜਾਨੀ ॥
ਨਾਨਕ ਦਾਸ ਸਦਾ ਕੁਰਬਾਨੀ ॥

Prelude to the Sikh Prayer :

Lord ! Thou art our Master, we pray to Thee.
Our body and soul were given by grace of Thee.
We art Thy children, Father and Mother are Thee.
All comforts we enjoy are bestowed by Thee.

Nobody can know how great are Thee.
Thou are superior-most, none superior to Thee.

Whole creation listens and obeys Thee.
Whoever is created abides by Thee.
Thy greatness is known only to Thee.
Nanak says, Thy pupils sacrifice their all to Thee.

PREFACE

1. Sikhism took birth in the East in Punjab, India, five centuries ago. Sikhs have settled all over the world not as conquerors of new lands, as the Europeans did four centuries ago, but as seekers of new opportunities in life. With them, the Sikhs carried their unique appearance and their unique philosophy. To the West, Sikhs migrated in the later part of the nineteenth century. Wherever they went, they established their gurdwaras (worship places). In the first two decades of this century gurdwaras were founded in Vancouver, Canada, Stockton, USA, and London, U.K, to name a few. Now almost all large cities in the West have a gurdwara; many have more than one.

Gurdwaras in North America formed their Sikh Council in 1979. They got together annually to discuss Sikh affairs in the West. In May 1984, the Council invited the author to give a lecture on Sikhism during its annual function in Los Angeles. Later the author moved to Washington, D.C., where he gave a series of discourses on basic principles of the Sikh faith in the gurdwara managed by the Guru Nanak Foundation of America. The author explained how the principles of the Sikh faith have been considered suitable by modern scholars for adoption by the whole of humanity. Some members of the congregation, desired that these lectures should be written in the form of a book for those who could not attend the gurdwara regularly.

The author was invited by many Sikh families to hold detailed discussions with Sikh youth. These discussions convinced him of the need for a small book describing the principles of the faith in terms, which were meaningful to the Western youth. These young people have little time to read long stories and details about the life of the Sikh Gurus. However, they are interested in understanding the development of the Sikh faith and its philosophy. They want to know how the Sikh philosophy can help them today in the Western environment and in a society, which emphasizes the scientific approach to every discipline. This book was written to meet their needs.

2. Another motivation for writing this book was an incidental

meeting with a man without a turban but bubbling with Sikh pride. It happened in 1979 at Gurdwara Baoli Sahib, Goindwal, Amritsar. The author was distributing religious literature at the stall of the Sikh Missionary College, Ludhiana. A visitor came straight to him and voluntarily narrated his story without a break and with indescribable emotion. What he said in Panjabi can briefly be translated as below :

I am also one of you, though I have cut my hair. I am the descendant of those Sikhs who went to Uttar Pardesh (U.P.) State during the 18th century to fight the repression let loose by the Mughal government. On the request of the local Hindus to protect them from the tyranny of the officials, our elders agreed to stay there. They spread themselves in many villages in that area. When the British East Indian Company defeated the Mughal government, this region came under the British rule. In the northwest beyond the river Sutlej. Maharaja Ranjit Singh ruled the Panjab State. After three or four generations, these settlers lost contact with their far away center, Amritsar, and they gave up their Sikh symbols. Our next, generations slowly adopted the rituals of the Hindus who were there in great majority. Now, only our name, Pachhadas or Westerners (Panjab is to the west of the U.P. state) differentiates us from the locals. Most of us still have faith in Sri Guru Granth Sahib and perform Sikh rites at the time of a birth, marriage or death in the family.

Pointing towards his 10-year-old son wearing a turban he concluded :

I have made my son a Sikh. If religious lectures are given in our area, a very large number of us are ready to return to the fold of the Sikh faith and adopt the Sikh symbols and the Sikh way of life. It gives me great solace to say that, if not we ourselves, at least our children will be able to know the greatness of their heritage and live as true Sikhs.

With rapt attention, the author heard this emotional description of the Sikhs in U.P. from a person longing to retrieve his lost heritage. The author is reminded of it every time when he comes across Sikh children without turbans. The strong fear, that most of the next Sikh generation in the West will be without Sikh symbols and that their children may know little of the Sikh faith, haunts the author all the time. Many Sikh parents in the West are constantly worried by the same thought. In fact they fear that the Sikh symbols will fall into disuse in the West even faster than in U.P. Many first-generation immigrants to Europe and America have already removed their Sikh symbols, while it were the third or fourth generation Sikhs who did so in U.P. The language barrier will further hasten this trend. Many Sikh children born in the USA, U.K. or Canada cannot read Gurbani; some cannot even speak Panjabi properly.

3. Instead of simply feeling alarmed by reading these observations, we should make efforts to check this trend. if we, the parents, the first and second generation immigrants, resolve to live as Sikhs and guide (not by force, but through education and example) our children to the Sikh way of life, we can feel assured that Sikhism will be retained as the religion of the future generations. This will bring peace not only to the Sikh youth but also to all those who come in contact with them.[1]

This book is, therefore, intended to explain the rationality of the Sikh faith and describe the high esteem in which the principles of Sikhism are held by the modern thinkers in the West. This knowledge will help stop the erosion of the Sikh faith taking place in the minds of the Western youth. Modern youth need to be educated to feel the urge for peace and pleasure of life explained in Sri Guru Granth Sahib. They also need to be told that Sikhs have a reputation as brave, fearless saint-soldiers (who defend rather than attack the rights of the weak), high class

---

1. Hundreds of North American Sikh youth trained at the Sikh heritage camps started in 1970, not only understand the greatness of their faith, but they can also explain it to their friends of European origin. They are happy to wear the Sikh symbols. Many of them now (1998) are doctors, professionals, engineers, teachers, etc. They act as good role models for other youth. They motivate other Sikh youth to enjoy the self-esteem of living like a Sikh and appearing like a Sikh. Many of them can recite, sing and interpret Gurbani. Further, they can also relate it to their lives. Though, there is no formal survey, but many people, based on their observations, agree that a higher percentage of North American youth can sing Gurbani than those in their homeland, Panjab.

sportsmen, top scientists, successful businessmen, excellent workers, faithful followers of the religion, and saviors of the poor helpless people. The knowledge of their glorious past will help the Sikh youth, presently not interested in their faith, to feel a sense of pride in being Sikhs. They will develop a desire to possess the virtues they inherited from their forefathers.

After comprehending Sikhism and its glory, young Sikhs may express their surprise in these words.

> *How great was Nanak! The humanity split by artificial barriers of caste, color, creed and different religions was united into a unique brotherhood. What a philosophy he gave! He says that anybody and everybody who loves God can realize Him. Further, a person can remember Him by any name, Allah, Ram, Gobind,God; all names are His. The Guru surely was much ahead of his time.*

4. By his present efforts for revitalizing Sikh thought in the West, the author is honoring a promise he made a long time ago. In 1949, when the author himself was young and studying at Khalsa College Amritsar, he listened to a lecture by Sant Teja Singh (Professor). He was sent by Sant Attar Singh of Mastuana to U.K. and other countries in 1905 to establish Sikh organizations there. Sant Teja Singh advised the Sikh youth to study the faith devotedly, attempt to live up to it and explain it to the youth in the West. The author was a member of the group of students who met the Sant after his lecture to seek guidance and training in taking up this responsibility. This effort to explain the glory of the Sikh faith is intended to fulfil the promise made by him in 1949.

A non-Sikh, interested in understanding Sikh philosophy and Sikh history, will also find this book quite useful and interesting. The author welcomes suggestions from the readers to make this book more useful and helpful for the Sikh youth and non-Sikh readers.

November 8, 2001   **Gurbakhsh Singh**
959, Phase IV
SAS Nagar
Chandigarh - 160 059

ACKNOWLEDGEMENTS

FIRST EDITION

The author is glad to thank all his friends who helped him prepare this book which introduces the basic principles of the Sikh faith to the Western youth. To mention only a few of the many names, I am obliged to Dr. Gurcharan Singh (Kalkat), Washington D.C. and Dr. Rajinder Singh (Bajwa), Washington, D.C., who motivated me, provided help and gave useful suggestions for completing the manuscript.

Thanks are due to S. Parampal Singh (Sidhu) Scotch Plains, N.J., for having the first draft typed and to his wife, Veronica, for advising some changes in it to make the draft more useful and acceptable to the Western youth. The author expresses his obligation to S. Gaginder Singh (Bowie), Maryland, who typed the revised draft and prepared the copy for editing.

Mrs. Judith Bali, Guelph, Ontario who kindly edited the draft deserves a lot of thanks. She wrote to the author, "I have changed a little of the grammar and have sometimes substituted words which I thought were more current among North American young people. Sometimes changing one word required a change in the whole sentence.... I have enjoyed your book very much, you have made Sikh history and philosophy very clear."

Mr. Manjit Singh (Sidhu), Editor World Sikh News kindly agreed to go through the manuscript and make improvements before the book was sent for type setting.

The credit for publishing and thus making the book available to the youth is due to The Sikh National Educational & Cultural Organization, Stockton, California.

SECOND EDITION

Thanks are due to all those who appreciated the contents of the book, first published under the title, "Sikhism, a faith for the modern man." The book has been revised and enlarged in view of the comments received from the readers.

Balpreet Kaur (Sandhu), Fredricksburg, Virginia, 7th grade student typed the draft. Ranjit Lal, Arlington, Texas, an

13

engineering student, transferred the text to his computer, made some useful changes in it and prepared manuscript for the editors.

Mrs. Ishnan Kaur, Mississauga, Ontario, and Mrs. Judith Bali, Guelph, Ontario, were requested for editing the book. They took lot of pains to critically examine the write up and correct it, they even rewrote some paragraphs afresh to convey the correct message to the readers. Because of their contributions they, in fact, have become co-authors of this book.

The job of planning the format and preparing the print copy was undertaken by Dr. Harbans Lal, Arlington, Texas. Typing of Gurbani quotations in Punjabi was arranged by the Canadian Sikh Study and Teaching Society, Vancouver.

THIRD EDITION

The book was critically read by many Sikh students of Greater Vancouver, Canada. They wanted me to revise it before printing the third edition. Jasjit Singh, Baldeesh Singh, Japjot Singh, Gurinder Singh, Kamalbir Singh of Vancouver and Jaskiran Kaur, Manvinder Singh, Sandeep Singh, Tarandeep Singh of Burnaby, Canada, made many changes and offered valuable suggestions. They all deserve the thanks of the author for their sincere efforts to make the book more useful to the readers.

Mantej Singh of Vancouver prepared the computer disk by scanning the second edition so that the book could be revised before reprinting. Baldeesh Singh and Jasjit Singh made the necessary corrections and other changes on the computer disk to prepare a revised draft. Mohinderpal Singh of Vancouver, Canada, made useful editorial contributions and typeset the final copy. All of them deserve the thanks of the author.

FOURTH EDITION

The fourth edition has been revised to include suggestions received from some readers; the author is sincerely grateful to all of them. Verpal Singh, a young Sikh of Kapurthala, Punjab, helped in the final editing of the manuscript for this edition.

Gurbakhsh Singh

14

CHAPTER I
SIKHISM FOUNDED

*Sikhism is a Universal World Faith, a message for
all men. This is amply illustrated in the writings of
the Gurus. Sikhs must cease to think of their faith as
just another good religion and must begin to think
of Sikhism being the religion for this New Age.*

This apt description of Sikhism was stated by Rev. H.L.
Bradshaw of the USA in the *Sikh Review*, Calcutta. Many others
have made similar observations about the Sikh faith, some of
which are cited in Chapter III of this book.

SOCIETY AND RELIGION
(A) ORIGIN OF RELIGIONS

The scientists believe that earlier humans lived like wild ▶
animals. They roamed the forests for food and inhabited along
the banks of rivers and lakes to meet their basic need of water.
They ate the leaves, roots and fruits of trees and plants. They
also consumed raw meat. The fossils reveal that hundreds of
thousands of years ago the oldest species walked on fours and
lived in trees. The first species which walked on twos was named
Homo erectus. Homo sapiens, the name given to the current
species of human beings, is considered to be the fourth
evolutionary stage.

With the development of the brain, there came an
improvement in the thinking power of the human beings. They
began to observe natural phenomena and began to interpret them.
It was obvious to them that their comforts were highly dependent
upon nature : rainfall, sun, wind, snow, etc. Accordingly, people
believed that there were 'super powers' who controlled their
lives and that they were beyond reach of the ordinary human
beings. Some of these powers made living comfortable while
others did the opposite. This led to a belief in many gods, favorable
or unfavorable towards mankind. In due course, people concluded
that there must exist the god of all the gods, the ultimate god;
today we call Him God.

The evolutionary process gave humans the knowledge of the three R's. Having acquired some faculties specific only to them, they perceived that a human being was not just another animal. Humans were definitely distinct from animals, even though their biological habits were similar. A line was thus drawn between animals and humans. This idea of distinguishing humans from animals, gave birth to the philosophy that there must be 'some purpose' to the human life. Only some special 'persons' could answer this riddle of life. Some gifted men answered this question. They were considered holy men or prophets; religion was thus born. It was universally agreed by such 'wise men' that one is a human being only if one lives to achieve the 'goal' of life. Otherwise a human lives the life of just another animal. With a spiritual goal in life, the 'animal human' changed into a 'divine human.'

Most of the religions are founded on the faith that there is God, Who alone is the Generator, the Operator and the Destroyer of this universe. The basic and fundamental characteristics of God mentioned by prophets of different religions are very similar. They differ, however, in the methods of worshipping and realizing God. The major differences lie in the rituals. This can be expected because of the differences in culture, and time period in which these religions originated and evolved.

(B) RELIGION, THE SOURCE OF MORAL AND SOCIAL VALUES

Human beings are called social animals. As a natural instinct, people want to live together in a society. Therefore, one has to know the proper and correct behaviour towards other members of society. Much before man formed regular governing institutions, called governments, religions gave the necessary guidance for the social and political behaviour of the people. Earlier, what was right or wrong (good or bad) was decided by the religious tenets, which later on formed the basis for our legal laws.

Religion offers a great advantage to society. It provides justification for the belief that a man should be honest and sincere and not a thief or a robber. Most religions tell us that all men are created by God, the Father. Being children of the same Father we are all equal like brothers and sisters. This philosophy, therefore, generates mutual goodwill and love among human beings.

16

Religion establishes what is necessary for a society to live in peace and prosperity. Society wants people to be honest, sincere, and affectionate towards each other. One is not expected to be a smuggler, a liar, or a cheat. One should neither think nor do anything that is antisocial. All such values are the extensions of the religious tenets. The government laws, having been set by man, are less respected. They are, therefore, more likely to be ignored than the religious directions. Religious commands are considered to be holy orders, and are, therefore, more respected than man-made laws.

In addition to these positive directions, religion provides a strong deterrent to evil thoughts. It asserts that ultimately we are accountable for all of our actions. Whereas we will surely be rewarded for our good deeds, we will have to suffer for all our bad acts. It is emphasized that man can cheat man but not the omnipresent and omniscient God. It is, therefore, desirable that society develops a faith in God for its own good.

(C) RELIGION, A SPIRITUAL PATH

Religion is actually much more than the above description given by philosophers and scientists. It is the extra-sensory experience or intuition of Truth with which holy persons are graced by God. It is almost impossible to explain this experience through worldly sciences. As an *idea* comes to the mind of a scientist so is the *spiritual thought* revealed to a holy person by God. They share that *"revelation"* with other people to guide their lives. We call their teachings religion.

(D) RELIGION, A DIVISIVE FORCE

There are many human races and ethnic groups on this earth. Different holy men founded religions on different lands inhabited by people with their individual cultures. With the passage of time, population increased and people moved from one land to another. Each community tried to subdue the other because of the residual animal character in man. As a result, hatred and ill will developed among the communities.

Further, whenever a new religion was founded in a land, people committed to older faiths resisted it. This opposition quite often resulted in wars within a community. Religion, which should have taught people to treat all humans as equals, acted as a divisive force. This happened not only between two different

17

ethnic groups, but also within the same community.

How to address God also became a controversial issue. The believers forgot that a father is a father, he may be addressed by any word, dad, daddy, or papa. Similarly God may be loved by any name, Allah, Gobind, God, Guru, Ram etc. Weak people were forced by those in power to change their Name of the God and method of prayer, all in the name of salvation. Refusal by the weak people to adopt the new faith meant their torture, harassment, and even murder by the rulers.

In India, one group of Hindus suffered at the hands of other Hindus. Brahmans considered themselves to be superior to all others. The so-called low caste, about one-sixth of the population, were considered untouchable and treated like animals. During the Muslim rule, the majority Hindu community suffered immensely. These were the conditions prevailing when **Guru Nanak Dev (1469-1539), the founder of Sikhism,** came on the scene.

A REVOLUTIONARY THOUGHT

(A) GOD LOVES ALL PEOPLE

(i) Nanak was born in village Talwandi (now Nankana Sahib, Pakistan). His father, Sri Kalu Ram, was the revenue official of the village. Chuharkana, a few kilometers away from the village, was the main marketing center for the region. It had a resting place for holy men moving around the country on pilgrimage tours. Whenever (Guru) Nanak, visited Chuharkana, he liked to discuss religious philosophies with the holy men there. He studied both in the Hindu Ashram and in the Muslim *madrassa* (school). After he had read the scriptures of these religions, (Guru) Nanak felt there could not be two separate Gods, Ram for the Hindus, and Allah for the Muslims as claimed by the people. He declared that there is only ONE GOD for whole humanity; He loves all people, irrespective of the name they may give to their faith. Further, we can love Him by any Name. (Guru) Nanak, therefore, preached that a believer of a faith should not be considered as a "non-believer" by the followers of the other faiths, just because he prefers to use a word of his own language for God.

This was a revolutionary idea in those days, and it gave new spiritual thought to the Muslim and the Hindu holy men visiting

18

Chuharkana. They carried this philosophy all over India on their pilgrimages and discussed it with other holy men. Because of his unique faith, (Guru) Nanak became well known not only in the Panjab but also in all regions of the Indian sub-continent including Sri Lanka.

(ii) Shri Kalu Ram did not appreciate the strong leaning of his son towards religious discourses and studies. Nor did he appreciate his son's habit of helping every needy person he saw, particularly, giving food and money to the travelling holy men. After (Guru) Nanak got married and became a family man, his father naturally felt that his son should be more interested in saving money rather than in spending it for the needy. The son, however, considered helping the needy to be a *Sacha Sauda*—a true bargain, the best use of his money. Finally, one day when (Guru) Nanak returned home after serving food to the fakirs (Gurdwara Sacha Sauda now stands there in his memory) resting at Chuharkana, his father became particularly angry. He took serious objection to (Guru) Nanak's spending money in that manner. Differences were reconciled when (Guru) Nanak agreed to move away from Talwandi and find a job elsewhere. His sister's husband, who was in the revenue department at Sultanpur Lodhi (District Kapurthala, Panjab), obtained for (Guru) Nanak the job of managing stores with the Nawab of the town.

(Guru) Nanak continued his habit of freely giving alms and participating in religious discourses. People who were jealous of his popularity complained that he was distributing some of the official stocks of grain in his custody. Twice the stores were inspected but nothing was ever found to be short. After the second inspection which was within a couple of years of his joining the service, Guru Nanak decided to declare the mission for which he had been sent by God.

(iii) One morning, as usual, he went to the nearby river for bathing, but this time, he did not return. All the people in the village started worrying about him. They presumed that he had drowned. However, on the third day, people were surprised to find him coming back to the village. The news spread like wild fire. Everyone including the Nawab, the ruler, was jubilant to see him back. They came running to him. When they asked where he had gone, (Guru) Nanak replied that he was called by the Almighty and he had brought a holy message for them from Him. He declared, "There is no Muslim, there is no Hindu (do not divide people into Hindus and Muslims), all are equal human beings because they are the children of the same Father, God." This is considered to be the first formal sermon of (Guru) Nanak.

After his historical visit to the river, he resigned his job, and put his wife and two children in the care of his father-in-law. He left Sultanpur to preach his newly-founded religion all over India and near-by countries. For this mission, he chose Mardana, a lowly Muslim, as his associate and called him *Bhai*, a brother. All through his arduous journeys Mardana played on rebeck, a string instrument, while Guru Nanak sang holy hymns. He met the heads of religious sects in India and in the Arabian countries to explain his message of one God and brotherhood of humanity. Religion was thus made a uniting force rather than a dividing force.

(B) BASIC PRINCIPLES

(i) Practice love, not hollow rituals

Guru Nanak went to a large number of Hindu religious places and met Pundits (scholars), Sidhs (who perform miracles), and Yogis. He told them that the mindless and hollow rituals done for exhibition had no value with God. They were like a counterfeit coin, which look genuine but is rejected because it does not contain the specified precious metal. Similarly, God rejects all rituals practiced by the people who have no sincere goodwill for other human beings.

There is no benefit to the soul from undergoing self-inflicted tortures such as abstaining from food, bathing in ice cold water, remaining surrounded by fire for a long time, keeping silent for long periods of time or standing continuously on one leg or in any other awkward posture. In those days Yogis and Sidhs performed such acts to claim their superiority over the common people and obtain contributions from them. Some are found doing similar acts even today.

The Guru did not approve of the belief that our ancestors, who are already dead, could be helped by giving alms to the Brahmans (the so-called high caste people). This was simply a means of some members of the priestly class to gain ascendancy over others. If this were acceptable to God, the rich would always

20

be guaranteed a better berth even in the next life. Guru Nanak made it categorically clear that people would be judged by their own deeds. They would not be benefitted by the rituals performed by their children or grandchildren. He said that people themselves are the abode of God. Therefore, He knows what is in our minds. One can cheat people but cannot cheat Him. Guru Nanak, therefore, preached that expressing sincere love and goodwill (not just for exhibition purposes only) towards other human beings was the surest way of obtaining peace here and hereafter.

(ii) Deeds alone are valued

Guru Nanak also visited many Muslim religious places including Mecca, Medina, Baghdad, and other shrines. The biggest question of those days, "Who is superior, a Muslim or a Hindu?", was asked of Guru Nanak by the Kazis (Muslim Judges). Guru Nanak's response, "Everybody without good deeds will repent"; satisfied everyone and could not be challenged or criticized by any of them.

ਪੁਛਨਿ ਫੋਲਿ ਕਿਤਾਬ ਨੋ ਹਿੰਦੂ ਵਡਾ ਕਿ ਮੁਸਲਮਾਨੋਈ?
ਬਾਬਾ ਆਖੇ ਹਾਜੀਆ ਸੁਭਿ ਅਮਲਾ ਬਾਝਹੁ ਦੋਨੋ ਰੋਈ ॥

(Bhai Gurdas Var 1-33)

Guru Nanak preached that God does not identify people by their sectarian religions such as Christians, Jews, Hindus or Muslims.In his hymns, he observed, "God judges us by our deeds and full justice is delivered to ever one in His court."

ਕਰਮੀ ਕਰਮੀ ਹੋਇ ਵੀਚਾਰੁ ॥ ਸਚਾ ਆਪਿ ਸਚਾ ਦਰਬਾਰੁ ॥

(Guru Granth, p. 7)

The Guru also said, *"For my spiritual guidance,, I do not believe in Hinduism or Islam and nor do I follow their rituals. My path is love for the Almighty, Who is the Lord of our bodies and souls. He is addressed as Ram by Hindus and Allah by Muslims."*

ਨਾ ਹਮ ਹਿੰਦੂ ਨ ਮੁਸਲਮਾਨ ॥ ਅਲਹ ਰਾਮ ਕੇ ਪਿੰਡੁ ਪਰਾਨ ॥

(Guru Granth, p. 1136)

God evaluates our deeds, and not merely our beliefs. The Guru made it clear that neither he nor any other prophet would be able to intercede at the time of final judgement, which would be based on actions only. Whether one was a king or a beggar, a so-called high-caste or a low-caste, belonged to one faith or the other, would make no difference in the final assessment. He wrote, "Any person who loves God realizes Him."

21

ਜਿਨੀ ਨਾਮੁ ਧਿਆਇਆ ਗਏ ਮਸਕਤਿ ਘਾਲਿ॥

ਨਾਨਕ ਤੇ ਮੁਖ ਉਜਲੇ ਕੇਤੀ ਛੁਟੀ ਨਾਲਿ॥   (Guru Granth, p. 8)

Guru Nanak also challenged the then prevailing, unfortunately it still exists, discrimination due to sex. Women were regarded as inferior and incomplete human being, and hence were given a very low status in society. A Hindu woman was not permitted to wear the religious thread (*Janju*). She was considered an obstacle in the path of God. That is why mystics, who wanted to devote their lives to realizing God, did not marry. Celibates, known as *Jatis,* were considered superior and were honored by the family men. Guru Nanak strongly disapproved of this thought. He asked how women could be rated inferior when they give birth to all men including the kings to whom people bow their heads.

ਸੋ ਕਿਉ ਮੰਦਾ ਆਖੀਐ ਜਿਤੁ ਜੰਮਹਿ ਰਾਜਾਨ॥

(Guru Granth, p. 473)

Nanak, therefore, showed the same respect to men and women and equally welcomed them to participate in all social and religious functions.

The hymns of Nanak and of all *Bhagats* (religious sages, devotees) stress the fact of the presence of God in every human being. They say that any act that hurts another person is wrong, because its displeases God residing in him. Any act, which helps the other person, is good because it is liked by God.

(iii) Live honestly

While on his preaching missions in Panjab, Guru Nanak once stayed with Bhai Lalo, an honest carpenter, instead of with the corrupt village official, Malik Bhago. Malik invited the whole village for a feast at his house but Guru Nanak did not attend. Malik called him and asked him to explain the reasons for not eating the sumptuous food served by him. Guru Nanak bluntly told him, in the presence of the respected village people, that it was "human blood" and not wholesome food that was being served to the people.

ਹਕੁ ਪਰਾਇਆ ਨਾਨਕਾ ਉਸੁ ਸੂਅਰ ਉਸੁ ਗਾਇ॥

(Guru Granth, p. 141)

ਜੇ ਰਤੁ ਲਗੈ ਕਪੜੈ ਜਾਮਾ ਹੋਇ ਪਲੀਤੁ॥

ਜੋ ਰਤੁ ਪੀਵਹਿ ਮਾਣਸਾ ਤਿਨ ਕਿਉ ਨਿਰਮਲੁ ਚੀਤੁ॥

(Guru Granth, p. 140)

Stunned by these fearless remarks, Malik demanded an explanation. The Guru told him, "If a cloth is stained by blood, we call it dirty. Your earnings are stained by the blood of the poor from whom you extract money illegally and forcibly. How can your mind be pious or clean ? It is only honestly earned money that is like the sweet milk, which I enjoy at the house of Bhai Lalo. Taking what is due to others is as sinful as pork is to a Muslim and beef to a Hindu." This awakened the sleeping soul of Malik. The Guru similarly exhorted Sajjan (nicknamed *Thag*), a robber and murderer living in the village of Tulumba in Multan, Pakistan, to earn his livelihood through honest means. He was also advised that one has to pay for one's actions in the end. Sajjan gave up his vices and became a true *sewadar* (service man) of the people.

(iv) Physical renunciation of no avail

Guru Nanak undertook an arduous journey to visit the Sidhs in the Himalayas. The Sidhs, who remain celibates, were surprised to see the Guru, a family man, there in the snowy mountains. They questioned him about the people down below in the plains. The Guru said, "The people are wondering who will protect them from evil. All the Sidhs, who obtained donations from them in return for promises of help and religious guidance, have run away to the snowy hills."

ਫਿਰਿ ਪੁਛਣਿ ਸਿਧ ਨਾਨਕਾ ਮਾਤ ਲੋਕ ਵਿਚਿ ਕਿਆ ਵਰਤਾਰਾ?....
ਸਿਧ ਛਪਿ ਬੈਠੇ ਪਰਬਤੀ ਕਉਣੁ ਜਗਤਿ ਕਉ ਪਾਰਿ ਉਤਾਰਾ ॥

(Bhai Gurdas, Var 1-29)

The ego of the Sidhs was cut down to size by this astute reply of the Guru. The Guru also exposed the Sidhs' hollow claim that remaining celibates made them better than married people. He asked them, "How dare you say that you are superior or are nearer to God than family men when you beg them for food and depend on them for your sustenance ?"

(v) Service is true worship

At Jagan Nath Temple, Puri, India, Guru Nanak told the priests that instead of worshipping the stone images of the gods, they should strive to become one with God's pervasive nature. The correct way to worship Him is to love other human beings who are His creation and in whom God actually resides.

Wherever Guru Nanak went, people greeted him in large

numbers and all leaders respected his new religious thought. He decried hollow, meaningless rituals and wanted people to realize God by observing His existence in every human being and everywhere in nature. Guru Nanak collected the writings of those Muslim *Pirs* and Hindu *Sants* who had also realized, that the same God is present in every human being. These hymns were later included in the Guru Granth under the title *Bhagat Bani* (hymns contributed by the devotees).

The technique Guru Nanak adopted to preach his faith can be understood from the above incidents (*Sakhis*) of his life. To learn more about the interesting and revealing incidents of the life of Guru Nanak, the reader may refer to one of the many books on this subject. For preaching his mission, Guru Nanak Dev spent about two decades visiting different religious places in India and adjacent countries.

GROWTH OF SIKHISM

The growth of Sikhism can be described under four major steps, *Sangat, Pangat, Sarovar* and Guru Granth, which were taken to reach the goal, the Guru Khalsa Panth. Guru Nanak laid the foundations of the faith by defining the path for his followers. His nine successors guided the disciples (Sikhs) to tread that path by themselves demonstrating how to stick to truth at the cost of their lives. The tenth Guru, bestowed the Guruship to the Sikhs who were committed to the mission and named them Guru Khalsa Panth. Now, the followers are popularly known as the Khalsa, the Panth, or the Sikhs.

(A) SANGAT AND PANGAT

Wherever Guru Nanak went, he established a *Sangat, a congregation,* in which all people, Hindus and Muslims, low caste and high caste, sit together as equals to sing the praises of the Almighty. One person was appointed as guide to each *Sangat* to conduct the religious discourses. The Guru also instituted *Pangat,* the sitting together as equals to partake of food, which was distributed free to everyone. Even today this practice of free (*Langar*) prevails in gurdwaras and reminds us that all human beings are equal and have the same rights.

After visiting major religious places of Hindus and Muslims in the Indian sub-continent and in the Arabian countries, Guru

Nanak settled at Kartarpur, now in Pakistan. It was a small village founded by him with the help of his father-in-law and his disciples. It is situated on the right bank of the river Ravi, opposite Dera Baba Nanak (Panjab, India). He lived there for about eighteen years, and demonstrated the value of *Sangat* and *Pangat*. Both Muslims and Hindus including the people of the so-called untouchable caste, attended his discourses. Irrespective of their caste, creed, economic status, sex or religion, all people were considered equal and were welcome to join the congregation. Religious discourses were held every morning and evening. The Guru preached that God loves all people; He is not the 'enemy' of any community. The claim of some religious leaders that only the followers of their faith would be 'saved' and others would be sent to Hell was wrong.

All people claimed Nanak as their own, a befitting testimony to his teachings. He was a *Pir* (religious leader) for the Muslims and a great Guru for the Hindus and the so-called low caste. Guru Nanak thus re-established the broken bonds of human brotherhood. Therefore, the following rhyme became a popular folklore :

Nanak Shah fakir, Hindu ka Guru Musalman ka Pir.

The significance of this social and spiritual revolution can be understood properly only when the then existing and still continuing mutual hatred among the communities and followers of different faiths is kept in mind. The Brahmans considered themselves to be superior to the rest of the Hindus. About one-sixth of the Hindus were treated as untouchables. The Muslims addressed the Hindus as *Kafirs* or non-believers. They did not allow the Hindus the same social and political rights that were available to the ruling Muslims. Hindus hated Muslims and called them *Malechh*, the un-pious foreigners. Muslims considered it a sacred act to harass and tease the Hindus and convert them to Islam, if necessary by force. It is this age of darkness that was enlightened by Guru Nanak, the 'Sun'.

ਸਤਿਗੁਰੁ ਨਾਨਕੁ ਪ੍ਰਗਟਿਆ ਮਿਟੀ ਧੁੰਧੁ ਜਗਿ ਚਾਨਣੁ ਹੋਆ ॥
ਜਿਉ ਕਰਿ ਸੂਰਜੁ ਨਿਕਲਿਆ ਤਾਰੇ ਛਪਿ ਅੰਧੇਰੁ ਪਲੋਆ ॥

(Bhai Gurdas, Var 1-27)

Guru Nanak, five centuries ago preached that the whole world is to be treated as one vast multi-cultural society. Mutual regard and respect among people were the foundation of the true religion. There was no religion superior to this. He said in Jap :

ਆਈ ਪੰਥੀ ਸਗਲ ਜਮਾਤੀ ਮਨਿ ਜੀਤੈ ਜਗੁ ਜੀਤੁ ॥

(Guru Granth, p. 6)

The person who accepts all humans as class-fellows (loves them as equals) is a holy person of the highest kind. One who controls his mind (and does not let it hate anyone) wins the world with love.

Now the world has formally accepted his preaching of equality of humans. The 30th anniversary of the Sharpeville massacre in South Africa, where peaceful demonstrators against apartheid were wounded and killed by their own government, was on March 21, 1990. In commemoration of this tragic event of 1960, the United Nations declared March 21 the International Day for the Elimination of Racial Discrimination.

Guru Nanak settled that the right to life, the right to equality, and the right to worship Him are God-given gifts to every person. No religious or political authority can take them away. One may praise God by any Name one wants to. (See also Chapter III)

The World Conference of Religions for Peace in 1979, actually endorsed the basic principles of the Sikh faith, when it, in its meeting in New Jersey, USA, concluded :

Too often the names and practices of our religions have been associated with warfare and strife. Now we must reverse this by :

(i) Breaking down barriers of prejudice and hostility between religious communities and institutions.

(ii) Confronting the powers of the world with the teachings of our religions rather than conforming to them when they act contrary to the well-being of humanity.

(iii) Building inter-religious understanding in our local community.

After the World War II, which shook the whole humanity and resulted in bloodshed all over the globe, most of the nations of the world got together and decided to form an organization of maintaining peace. It was named United Nations Organization and located in New York, USA. For assuring peace in the future they passed the Bill of Human Rights in 1949. When the teachings

26

of Guru Nanak are studied in the light of this Bill they are found to be a crusade for protecting the rights of the weak and lowly. His successors, as will be seen from the next pages, stood against the tyrant rulers. They sacrificed their lives to assure such rights, as listed in the Bill, to all people irrespective of their faith.

Before Guru Nanak passed away in 1539, he appointed Bhai Lehna as the Second Nanak and re-named him Guru Angad Dev.

Guru Angad Dev (1504-1552), the second Nanak

He lived in the village of Khadur, situated on the right bank of the river Beas and a few kilometers upstream from the *pattan* or ford on the highway that connected Delhi with Lahore. His father, a shopkeeper, was an ardent devotee of the Jwala Mukhi Devi in the Kangra hills. After the death of his father, he started leading the pilgrims to visit the Devi temple. It was during one of his journeys to the temple of the Devi that he was struck with the desire to meet Guru Nanak as well. After hearing the Guru's discourses, Bhai Lehna felt that he had found what he had wanted in his life. In 1532 he handed over his business to his nephew and made him the head of the family. Bhai Lehna left Khadur to stay at Kartarpur so that he could enjoy singing His virtues, *Hari Kirtan* and the divine environment. He learnt and practiced the principles of the Sikh faith under the guidance of the Guru for seven years. Finally, he was chosen as the second Nanak and directed to move to Khadur Sahib, the place of his original residence, to establish another Sikh center there.

Guru Angad Dev carried on the preaching of the Sikh principles through the practice of *Sangat* and *Pangat* at this new center. He made Sikhism popular with the common villagers of the region. He started centers for teaching Gurmukhi, the script in which Gurbani hymns were written. He appointed Baba Amar Das, aged seventy-two years and older than he by about twenty-five years, as his successor, the third Nanak.

Guru Amar Das (1479-1574), the third Nanak

He came to Khadur Sahib at the age of sixty and served there for twelve years with great devotion and sincerity. His love for doing the arduous job of preparing and serving *Langar* won the hearts of the *Sangat* and Guru Angad Dev. Before being chosen as the third Guru, Baba Amar Das was deputed to establish a third Sikh Center, a few kilometers downstream from Khadur Sahib. The place belonged to a person known as Gonda. He donated the land to the Guru and requested him to build a preaching center there. The new center was, therefore, named Goindwal Sahib.

To further strengthen the human bonds, Guru Amar Das constructred a *Baoli*, an open well with steps leading to the water. He welcomed everyone, the Muslims, the Hindus, and the so-called untouchables, to take water from the *Baoli* so that the artificial barriers of sect and caste among the people could be destroyed. Thus, the fragile human bonds were regenerated and strengthened. The Guru established additional preaching centers which were called *manjis*. The preachers sat on a cot, *manji*, while giving *sermons* to the *Sangat*. A Muslim, Allah Yar Khan, was in charge of one of these *manjis*. Women were also welcome for this honorable assignment. A team of husband and wife, Matho and Murari, earned great reputation as Sikh preachers.

To integrate the so-called low caste with the rest of the population, the third Nanak made *Pangat* a pre-condition for *Sangat*. In other words, he made it obligatory for all persons to sit together and partake of food in *Langar* before they were allowed to attend the congregational meetings and prayers. This removed the inferiority complex of the low caste people and the so-called untouchables. It simultaneously depleted the vanity of the rich and high caste people. This was necessary if mutual bonds of human feeling were to be developed among all sections of society.

Some high caste people, finding the institutions of *Pangat* and *Sangat* a great blow to their prestigious social status, started creating problems for the Guru. Local henchmen were hired by them to intimidate and harass the Sikhs visiting the Guru. The high castes went to the extent of lodging a formal complaint with the Emperor Akbar, who was nearby at Lahore. Their major objection was that the Guru was desecrating the Hindu faith by permitting the untouchables to sit and eat along side the higher castes. Akbar summoned the Guru to Lahore to give his reply to the charges levelled against him by the high caste persons.

Bhai Jetha, later Guru Ram Das, was sent to refute the charges against the Guru. After listening to the Guru's emissary,

28

the emperor not only rejected the memorandum of the deputation, but even paid homage to the Guru by visiting Goindwal. Before meeting the Guru, Akbar himself had to observe the rules of the *Pangat*, partaking of food sitting alongside ordinary people. He was so pleased with the institution of the *Pangat* that he wanted to donate a *Jagir* (income from a unit of villages) for the expenses of *Langar*. The Guru declined the offer stating that to remain a community affair, *Langar* had to be run out of the voluntary contributions of the disciples, not from the donations of the emperor.

(B) AMRIT SAROVAR

Guru Amard Das established another preaching center, which later became the headquarters of the Sikh faith. The requisite piece of land, encompassing a low-lying pond surrounded by natural vegetation, was chosen in 1570. The land belonged to the villages of Gumtala, Sulanwind, Gilwali, and Tung.

For this site, the Guru envisioned an *Amrit Sarovar*, a pool open to people of every caste, creed, faith or status. In the center of the pool, the Harimandar (later popularized by the British as the Golden Temple), was to be constructed where in nothing but God's virtues were to be sung.

After obtaining the land and preparing the layout plans and designs, Bhai Ram Das, popularly known as Jetha Ji, the son-in-law of the Guru, was deputed for this task. Before the Guru passed away, he named **Bhai Ram Das (1534-1581) as the fourth Nanak.** The digging and construction work continued throughout the life of Guru Ram Das. The city was formally founded in 1577 when buildings of clay huts, which were to be used as residential places, was started on the site purchased by the Guru.[1]

Now the place is known as Gurdwara Guru Ke Mahal. People came from far and near to perform voluntary service and offered their contributions for this holy center, first named Chak Ram Das, then Ram Das Pur. The Guru named his third son, Arjun Dev, as the fifth Nanak.

---

1. In 1577 he (Guru Ram Das) acquired the site along with 500 bighas (about 100 acres) of land on payment of 700 Rupees to the Zemindars of village Tung, who owned the land. —*The Amristar Gazetteers 1883-1884.*

Guru Arjun Dev (1563-1606), the fifth Nanak

Guru Arjun Dev continued the construction work. The foundation stone of the Harimandar, the sanctum sanctorum in the center of the pool, was laid in 1589. The whole complex was erected with the voluntary labor of the devotees from all over the Indian sub-continent and the offerings made out of their hard earned frugal savings. It was the yearnings for the love of their Lord, which made the Sikhs to offer their Tan, Man and Dhan (body, mind and earnings), that is, everything they had, was offered to the Guru. The edifice, which emerged from such a pious labor and holy contributions, offers the visitors an inspring faith and unshakable confidence in the benevolence of the Almighty.

Bhai Salo, a devotee of the Guru, with the efforts of his various friends and influential relatives, brought people of various skills and professions from all over the Panjab. It is said that people of 52 different trades were provided the necessary facilities to start their work in Chak Ram Das.

The *Sarovar* was built at a low lying place where a small natural lake already existed. The water level in the lake depended upon the rainfall received during the year. Whenever the rainfall was low the pool used to get almost dry. The Sikhs, therefore, decided to make some arrangements for assured water supply to the tank. They dug a small canal called Hansli to draw water from the river Ravi. The water started flowing in 1791. About two centuries later, in 1982 a pipeline from a nearby regular canal was built for providing water to the *Sarovar*.

When the work neared completion, there was a great famine in the region. Small-pox struck the public simultaneously. The money received from the disciples for the construction work was diverted to help the hungry, the sick, the needy, and the orphaned. The Guru himself toured the afflicted areas. He lived with the people, encouraging them and helping them in every manner. The Guru's own son, Har Gobind, was also afflicted with smallpox. Luckily his life was saved. Later he became the sixth Nanak.

The people and the government administrators were moved by the selfless work done by the Guru to alleviate their sufferings. The Faujdar or Administrator of Jalandhar, impressed by these acts of the Guru, requested that he help the people in the Jalandhar area as well and establish a Sikh center in his region. Accordingly, the Guru founded a new town, Kartarpur, fifteen kilometers from Jalandhar on the main road towards Amritsar. The town of Tarn Taran, about twenty kilometers to the south of Amritsar, was also built by the Guru. A huge pool and a gurdwara were also constructed there. This gurdwara served as a center for caring for the sick, the old and the orphaned.

(C) SRI GURU GRANTH SAHIB

Guru Arjun Dev not only vigorously practiced and preached the already established three principles of *Sangat, Pangat* and *Sarovar,* but he also took a fourth major step. He compiled the sacred scripture, Sri Guru Granth Sahib. This provided a common Holy Scripture for all sections of society. It helped to unite them into one unique brotherhood having faith in one common God with many names.

Sri Guru Grant Sahib was the first religious scripture of its kind. In addition to the Gurus, its contributors include many holy men from all over India, such as Kabir, a low caste weaver, Farid, a Muslim holy man, Ravidas, a shoe-maker from Varanasi, Namdev, a low caste calico printer and others. The only criterion for selecting a contributor was his belief that the same God exists in every human being, a philosophy emphasized by the Guru. (Chapter III)

ਅਵਲਿ ਅਲਹ ਨੂਰੁ ਉਪਾਇਆ ਕੁਦਰਤਿ ਕੇ ਸਭ ਬੰਦੇ ॥
ਏਕ ਨੂਰ ਤੇ ਸਭੁ ਜਗੁ ਉਪਜਿਆ ਕਉਨ ਭਲੇ ਕੋ ਮੰਦੇ ॥

(Guru Granth, p. 1349)

God is the Father of us all; His reflection is in everyone of us, hence do not grade any person as inferior or superior.

ਇਕੁ ਫਿਕਾ ਨਾ ਗਾਲਾਇ ਸਭਨਾ ਮੈ ਸਚਾ ਧਣੀ ॥
ਹਿਆਉ ਨ ਕੈਹੀ ਠਾਹਿ, ਮਾਣਕ ਸਭ ਅਮੋਲਵੇ ॥
ਸਭਨਾ ਮਨ ਮਾਣਿਕ ਠਾਹਣੁ ਮੂਲਿ ਮਚਾਂਗਵਾ ॥
ਜੇ ਤਉ ਪਿਰੀਆ ਦੀ ਸਿਕ ਹਿਆਉ ਨ ਠਾਹੇ ਕਹੀ ਦਾ ॥

(Guru Granth, p. 1384)

If you love God and wish to please Him do not utter a single harsh word. Further, do not hurt the feelings of anyone, the Lord is there in every heart.

31

ਸਭੇ ਘਟ ਰਾਮੁ ਬੋਲੈ ਰਾਮਾ ਬੋਲੈ ॥ ਰਾਮ ਬਿਨਾ ਕੋ ਬੋਲੈ ਰੇ ॥

(Guru Granth, p. 988)

In every heart there is God, none else than He speaks from there.

Sri Guru Granth Sahib offered a radically new outlook and philosophy to the people. It taught them that realizing or perceiving God was not restricted to the high classes or castes only. The inclusion of the hymns written by *Bhagats* or holy men belonging to the so-called low castes proved that any person, whatever his birth or faith, could become a holy man. Guru Nanak also revealed that no community or an individual has a monopoly on God and no one can claim to the sole representative of God on earth.

The Guru observed that differences in language, culture, and appearance are related to the differences in environment. All these variations are superficial differences and not inequalities. Human emotions in all people are the same. People have their own local languages and culture; hence there are different words for praising God and different rituals towards Him. Therefore, one community should not discriminate against the other because of such differences.

The Gurus accepted all the prevailing names of God, such as Allah, Ram, Gobind, Bhagwan, Rahim and Karim, as equally valid, and all of them were used in hymns for addressing God. All languages such as Arabic, Persian, Panjabi, Hindi, Sanskrit, and local dialects were equally acceptable for singing God's praises, and were included in Sri Granth Sahib.

To bring together the people of the two opposing (mutually hating) faiths, the Hindus and the Muslims, the Gurus used their religious terms jointly in rhyme, for example, *Ved-Kateb, Ram-Rahim, Puran-Quran.* The Harimandar Sahib and the *Sarovar* were open to all people irrespective of their caste and faith. This was in total contrast to the then prevailing barriers between Hindus and Muslims. Mosques were out of bounds for Hindus, and Hindu temple authorities did not permit Muslims or low caste people to worship there.

The Guru established another new tradition. Instead of erecting a stone image of Guru Nanak in the Harimandar, he installed there Sri Granth Sahib, to perpetuate the philosophy of the Shabad (Word) and Gian (Knowledge) Guru.

So far we have found that the Gurus took revolutionary steps to reunite the split society. They preached that all humans had equal rights and any section of them could not be considered high or low because of their birth. A person could not be called a non-believer simply because a different name was used by him to sing the praises of God. Rather, anyone who wished to realize God should first love to be a member of the human brotherhood.

Sikhism, because of its principles and the vigorous preaching by the Gurus, was acceptable to all people. This mass acceptance of the faith by the common people made Sikhs a potential social and political force. The erosion of the Muslim faith surprised Muslim leaders and they began to consider Sikhism a challenge to their faith and political power. The Muslim government, therefore, tried to suppress Sikhs and the spread of their faith.

CHAPTER II
REPRESSION OF THE SIKH FAITH

In about a century, Sikhism had become a mass movement. Even some Muslims who enjoyed a privileged position in the State embraced Sikhism. For example, Mian Mir, a well-known Muslim, became a disciple of the fifth Nanak, Guru Arjun Dev. The rulers found it difficult to tolerate the growth of Sikhism and its ever-increasing popularity. The reaction of the Muslim leaders to these developments is found in the diary of the Emperor Jahangir. He wrote, *"For a long time I wanted to close this shop of falsehood* (the Sikh preaching center) *because not only Hindus but also unwary Muslims were becoming disciples of Arjun. I, therefore, ordered the killing of the Guru."*

The persecution of Guru Arjun Dev was brought about with the connivance of the Guru's elder brother, Prithi Chand,.who was staking his claim to the Guruship. The governor of Lahore permitted two armed attacks on Amritsar to kill or at least dislodge the Guru and install his stooge, Prithi Chand, as Guru. Both times, the attempts failed. In the first case, the Commander Sulhi Khan was charred to death when his horse reared and jumped into a live brick-kiln. The second attempt failed because the Commander was beheaded by his own servant the night before the attack.

The Guru realized that violent intervention in his program would not subside. Sikhism, inspite of its emphasis on peace and tolerance, was perceived by the Muslim leaders as a threat to their supremacy. Therefore, to ensure that Sikhism could withstand such onslaughts, Guru Arjun Dev trained his son Har Gobind, in martial arts.

The policy not to harass Hindus adopted by Emperor Akbar, was not approved by the Muslim clergy in India or in Mecca. They wanted a ruler who would let loose terror on non-Muslims in India and force them to either convert or to live a degraded life as slaves. Jahangir, the son of Akbar, adopted this fanatic policy. The Guru was falsely accused of helping the emperor's opponents. He was summoned to Lahore where he was submitted to excruciating torture and killed by pouring scorching sand on his head. His body was consigned to the Ravi on May 30, 1606.

Guru Har Gobind (1595-1644), the sixth Nanak

After the martyrdom of his father, Guru Har Gobind wore two swords, one symbolizing *Piri*, and the other symbolizing *Miri*. They respectively represent divinity and worldly leadership. It was a signal to the rulers that the Guru would defend the religious and human rights, if need be, even with sword. In 1609, in front of the gate of the Harimandar Sahib, he laid the foundation of the Akal Bunga; it was a seat to oversee the social welfare of the down-trodden. The Harimandar provided a place for enjoying the divine love and obtaining the required spiritual strength for serving the people. The Guru invited young men to come to Amritsar with horses and arms to be trained to protect human rights and the faith of the people in times of emergency. Popularity of this step can be judged from the fact that a Muslim named Painde Khan served as one of the commanders of the Guru's defense forces.

ARMY ATTACKS

In an attempt to stem the rising popularity of Sikhism, Emperor Jahangir arrested the Guru and sent him to Gwalior, a town far away from Panjab. However, the great respect of the masses for the Guru forced Jahangir to set the Guru free. The Guru refused to leave the fort, unless the fifty-two princes, the rulers of small kingdoms imprisoned there, were also set free. Jahangir had no alternative but to agree to that. As a result of this episode, people began to call the Guru *'Bandi Chhore'*, savior of the prisoners.

After some time the repression started again. They army of the governor of Lahore attacked the Guru three times. In addition, the forces of the Faujdar of Jalandhar challenged the Guru's people in a scuffle. Every attack was repulsed by the Guru. Consequently, the plans of the Mughal ruler to kill the Guru and destroy the Sikh faith misfired. The Mughals lost their prestige as invincible soldiers. The Sikhs became even more confident of their physical ability to protect the people. Sikhism became more popular after the Sikhs defeated the Mughal soldiers. The first battle took place in 1628 when Amritsar was attacked by the forces of the governor of Lahore. A Muslim historian, Mohsin

Fani, witnessed the last battle at Kartarpur. He wrote "Throughout the battle the Guru's face showed only sublime disinterest far above the base emotions of anger and desire for revenge often associated with war."

THE NEW CENTER, KIRATPUR

To avoid armed clashes with the government forces, Guru Har Gobind left Amritsar and moved to Kiratpur, a small village in the foot hills of the Himalayas and situated on the left bank of the river Sutlej. He established a new center there for preaching Sikh faith. It was quite far away from Lahore and Sirhind, the Muslim administrative centers. Before leaving this world, he nominated his grandson as his successor. None of the four Gurus, who succeeded him, returned to Amritsar to live in the holy city. To conduct their campaign for human rights, they had to fight against the belligerent Mughals and their satraps on a land away from Amritsar.

Guru Har Rai (1630-1661), the seventh Nanak

He carried on the preaching of the faith in the new regiuns. People from as far as Assam and Bangla Desh in the east, and Afghanistan in the west, visited him to seek spiritual guidance. They presented their offerings for the support of his mission. The Guru maintained a military posture but tactfully tried to avoid any armed clash with the rulers.

Aurangzeb won the battle fought among the brothers for the throne of Delhi. To assure the throne for himself, he committed many infamous acts. He executed his brothers and arrested his father. To improve his image and present himself as a first rate puritan, he unleashed terror not only against non-Muslims but also against liberal and Sufi Muslim fakirs. The celebration of Muharram by Shia Muslims was banned and many Shia priests were executed. The leader of Bohra Muslims and his 700 followers were killed. Many famous Muslims saints (Hussain, Sarmad, Qualandar, etc.), scholars and holy men not following the Sunni code of conduct lost their lives. The tortures and killings ordered by Aurangzeb are far too many to be listed here.

In Panjab, he intensified the policy of terrorizing the Sikhs and subjugating the Guru. He thought of calling the Guru to Delhi and then publicizing the meeting to create the false image that the Guru had submitted himself to the emperor. The Guru, instead of going himself, sent his elder son, Ram Rai with a couple of his disciples. The meetings between Ram Rai and Aurangzeb turned out to be quite friendly. Aurangzeb listened to Ram Rai's religious discourses. The emperor expected Ram Rai to become the next Nanak and hoped to mould the preaching of Sikhism to suit his plans.

The *Maulvis* (Muslim priests) did not like Aurangzeb's close relationship with the son of the Guru. Hoping to force Ram Rai to make a statement against Muslims, they asked Ram Rai to explain a hymn in Sri Guru Granth Sahib.

ਮਿਟੀ ਮੁਸਲਮਾਨ ਕੀ ਪੇੜੈ ਪਈ ਕੁਮ੍ਿਆਰ ॥
ਘੜਿ ਭਾਂਡੇ ਇਟਾ ਕੀਆ ਜਲਦੀ ਕਰੇ ਪੁਕਾਰ ॥

(Guru Granth, p. 466)

The couplet refers to the futility of the Muslim practice of burying a body to save it from being burnt. In due course of time, the body decays and becomes part of the soil. Pots made from that soil may be put in the fire for preparing burntclay pots. Ram Rai said, "The word is not *Musalman* but *Bayeeman* or dishonest man." This explanation satisfied the emperor and the *Maulvis*, but it was against the Sikh teachings. The Guru took serious note of the selfish motives of his son, who compromised religious principles for the sake of his worldly friendship. The emperor gave him a *Jagir* (real estate) in Dehradoon. (This estate is still with the present successors of Ram Rai.) The Guru cast his son out of the Sikh faith, and forbade his disciples to have any dealings with him. The emperor had wanted to use Ram Rai to create dissension among the Guru's followers.

Guru Hari Krishan (1656-1664), the eighth Nanak

Guru Har Rai passed on the Guruship to his younger son, Hari Krishan, who was only five years old at the time. He too was called to Delhi through a subtle move. The emperor's minister, Raja Jai Singh, a devoted disciple, invited the Guru to his bungalow (where now stands Gurdwara Bangla Sahib) and treated him with great honor. Aurangzeb sent a message to the Guru that he wanted to meet the Guru. In fact, Aurangzeb planned to stage this meeting in such a way that Guru Har Krishan would appear to be submitting to the emperor. The Guru understood and refused to comply. Even when Aurangzeb offered to come to the Guru's bungalow, he declined to meet him. The emperor felt insulted but was helpless. He tried to wash away this insult by stating that he himself had nothing to do with the "child" but that his son wanted to play with him. To make his story believable, he sent his son, Bahadur Shah, to the bungalow of the Guru to play with him.

At that time, smallpox was raging in the city. The Guru personally went to see the people suffering from this disease which had taken a heavy death toll. Because of his continued exposure to the disease, he himself was infected and was unable to recover. He nominated his grand uncle as the ninth Nanak by stating, "*Baba Bakale.*" By these words, he referred to Tegh Bahadur, his grandfather's brother living in the village of Bakala near Amritsar.

Guru Tegh Bahadur (1621-1675), the ninth Nanak

The inauguration of Guru Tegh Bahadur was delayed to frustrate the emperor. It was to send a clear signal to him that he cannot thrust a Guru on the Sikhs. Aurangzeb's supporters took advantage of this delay to project Ram Rai as Guru, but they failed because the people did not accept him. Furthermore, many elder relatives of the Guru living at Kartarpur also claimed the Guruship. They travelled to Bakala and camped there so that they would appear to be inhabitants of Bakala and thus conforming to the words of the late Guru. Each claimant hired agents to solicit public support. None of them could convince the Sikhs of his being the Guru. They all were recognized as pretenders and rejected. Finally, the *Sangat* of Delhi with the guidance of Makhan Shah Lobana, formally declared Guru Tegh Bahadur as the ninth Nanak. The agents of Dhirmal, (who had the possession of the original volume of Sri Granth Sahib, compiled by the fifth Nanak) had the strongest claim to the Guruship. He tried unsuccessfully to assassinate the Guru.

(I) PREACHING IN THE EAST

The ninth Nanak had the difficult task of dealing with a hostile government. He purchased Makhowal village from the hill raja of Bilaspur and built another Sikh center there which he made his new headquarters. It is situated a few kilometers upstream from Kiratpur on the left bank of the river Sutlej. The place was first named Chak Nanaki and later became known as Anandpur Sahib.

His only child, Gobind Rai, was born at Patna in 1666 when

38

the Guru, along with his family, was travelling to the east. The son and his mother stayed there for about five years. Guru Tegh Bahadur toured the eastern regions of the Indian subcontinent going as far as Bengal and Assam. When in Assam, the Guru reconciled the differences between the local tribal ruler and the army of the emperor of Delhi.[1] This avoided the impending battle between them and saved many innocent lives. In memory of this service by the Guru, the armies of the local raja and of the emperor of Delhi raised a big mound or *dhobari* as a monument to him. The Gurdwara Dhobari Sahib now stands there.

(II) CONVERSION IN KASHMIR

Meanwhile, Muslim rulers particularly in Kashmir intensified their efforts to convert Hindus to Islam. The Guru heard about this harassment and killing of Hindus. He hastily returned to Panjab. A deputation of Kashmiri Brahmans visited Anandpur Sahib. They reminded the Guru that their ancestors had depended on the sixth Nanak to protect them from Emperor Jahangir. They reiterated that to save themselves and their faith they had no one else to turn to but the Guru. The Guru after hearing of the atrocities committed against them assured them of his support and protection. He told them to inform the Muslim ruler that instead of coercing so many Hindus he should convert the Guru to Islam. As they all follow the Guru, they would automatically adopt Islam.

Because of the forcible conversions, the countryside was in a state of terror. The Guru went from one place to another encouraging the frightened people to lead honest and upright lives. He toured Malwa, the tract to the southeast of river Sutlej, which today includes parts of the present day Panjab, Haryana and Rajasthan. Thousands of people would gather to hear the Guru, as he represented hope in their lives. To help them face the threatening environment, Guru's message to them was : *Fear none, frighten none; Love the Lord Mighty One.*

ਭੈ ਕਾਹੂ ਕਉ ਦੇਤ ਨਹਿ ਨਹਿ ਭੈ ਮਾਨਤ ਆਨ ॥

(Guru Granth, p. 1426)

---

1. The political problem between the Delhi government and the local Assamese again became serious after 1947 when India became free. It continues to be the cause of bloodshed even today.

The emperor was angered after hearing of the Guru's reply to the Kashmiri deputation. This time, instead of calling the Guru to Delhi (as he did in the case of the seventh and the eighth Gurus), he ordered his arrest.

(III) EXECUTION OF THE GURU

The Guru was taken to Delhi where he was put in the custody of the police. The emperor ordered the torture of the Guru and his associates to force them to accept Islam. The Guru argued, "Everyone, as a matter of his birthright, is free to remember God the way he likes. This right cannot be taken away by the king." Having failed to force the Guru and his followers to give up their faith, the emperor directed the officials to torture them to death. Bhai Mati Das was split into two by a saw and Bhai Dyala was boiled to death in water. Bhai Sati Das was wrapped in cotton and burnt alive. The head of the Guru was cut off with a sword. Thousands of Delhi citizens were forced to watch these horrifying acts. Gurdwara Sisganj stands by the side of the kotwali or Police Station[1] where the Guru was imprisoned and where he was beheaded.

The head of the Guru was secretly taken to Anandpur Sahib by Bhai Jaita. Lakhi Shah Vanjara, a trader, took the headless body to his camp and cremated it by setting fire to his cottage to conceal what he was doing, from the emperor's men. Gurdwara Raqab Ganj was built there by Sardar Baghel Singh when he conqurered Delhi about a century after the martyrdom of the Guru.

The cold-blooded murder of the Guru and his associates in 1675 sent a wave of intense emotional anger among the scared and frightened people throughout India. The public united to fight this *zulam* or cruelty. This resistance did not subside till Aurangzeb, exhausted from quelling the rebellions in his kingdom, died in 1707. Before dying the confessed in a letter to his sons, "I am leaving with empty hands. I collected sins all my life. I am frightened to see my death nearing. After my death, there will be riots everywhere."

Guru Gobind Singh (1666-1708), the tenth Nanak

Guru Tegh Bahadur's only child, Gobind Rai, was nine years

---

1. Recently this historical place has been handed over to the Sikhs to build a memorial to the Guru.

old when the great responsibility of directing the affairs of the Sikh faith fell on shoulders. Armed repression of the Sikh movement by the frustrated emperor was highly probable. The Sikhs had to be prepared to face that eventuality. The Guru, therefore, declared, "When all peaceful methods fail to change the mind of the wicked, it is justified to pick up the sword to save one's honor."

Sikhs were invited to Anandpur Sahib with arms and horses. They were given training in self protection. Unfortunately, the Hindu rajas in the nearby hills of Himachal did not like to see the Guru's increasing popularity with the common people. They started finding excuses to fight with the Guru and weaken him.

Since the Guru wanted to avoid any confrontation with the rajas, he worked to develop good relations with them. He visited the kingdom of Sirmur on the invitation of the Raja, and thus honored the traditional culture of the rajas. The Guru founded a new center, Paonta Sahib, which he built on the bank of the river Jamna. He invited scholars and poets to this place and encouraged them to read their compositions before the *Sangat*. A center for great learning was thus established there. The Guru stayed at Paonta for several years and had classical literature translated into Panjabi for the benefit of the people. There were more than 50 scholars engaged by the Guru for this purpose. The Guru himself wrote hymns for the Sikhs and they were later included in a compilation along with the writings of the poets now named Dasam Granth. Guru Gobind Singh Foundation has now built a Writers House at Paonta Sahib as a monument to the Guru. Scholars of every faith are welcome to stay there, enjoy the perfect natural setting on the banks of the river and write creative literature for propagating peace.

A battle was forced on the Guru by the rajas, while he was busy in the religious and academic activities at Paonta far away from his headquarters, Anandpur Sahib. The Sikhs, with local resources won this battle. It was fought near Bhangani village, a few kilometers upstream from Paonta. After this, the Guru returned to Anandpur Sahib to continue preaching Sikhism and training Sikhs in martial arts.

Within a year after forcing the battle near Bhangani on the Guru and losing it, the rajas found themselves in great trouble. They had to face a confrontation with the Muslim commander of

Kashmir who came with a big army to obtain money from them. They had no alternative but to request help from the Guru. The Guru willingly agreed to protect them, ignoring their attack on his Sikhs at Paonta. He wanted to save people from the pending danger. The Muslim commander was defeated and he escaped at night. The rajas were very much relieved to get rid of the invader. However, in their hearts they were frightened of the fighting skills and martial strength of the Sikhs. They feared the Guru could conquer them any time he wanted.

The Guru encouraged the hill rajas to cease being "slaves" of the Mughals and to declare their independence, but the rajas did not dare antagonize the mighty Mughal empire. The battle at Paonta and the battle against the Muslim commander of Kashmir had injured the pride of both the Rajputs and Mughals. Their reputations as great fighters were no longer secure, since the Sikhs, many of whom came from the "weak" low castes, had proved themselves to be the masters of the battlefield. Accordingly, the Mughals and the rajas decided to jointly attack the Guru and destroy his strength.

Dault Rai Arya studied these facts thoroughly and about a century ago wrote a book, *Sahib-e-Kamal, Guru Gobind Singh* in Urdu. He observed that had those ungrateful rajas joined the Guru, India would have gotten its freedom from the Mughal rulers before the end of the 17th century. Because of their fear of the Mughals, the ungrateful rajas turned against the Sikhs and they sided with the emperor in an attempt to kill the Guru and to finish the Sikh movement.

(I) GURUSHIP TO THE KHALSA

In 1699, Guru Gobind Rai called a special gathering of the Sikhs on Baisakhi Day. In front of the gathered Sikhs, he raised his naked, glittering sword and announced that he wanted a Sikh to offer his head to protect righteousness. He made this demand five times and five Sikhs, one by one, came forward to offer their heads to the Guru. They were given *Amrit* by him and addressed as *Panj Pyaras* "The Five Beloved Ones." *The Guru then requested these five Singhs to give Amrit to him to make their first 'disciple'.* After taking *Amrit*, the Guru became Gobind SINGH (Chapter IV). The Guru thus passed on the Guruship not to another individual, but to the corporate body of the Sikhs, and named it the Guru Khalsa Panth. The Guru himself became the first member of this body. There was no chance that this Guru Khalsa, the corporate body, could ever be killed or eliminated.

The miracle had happened. People divided as Hindus, Muslims, low caste, and high caste were united as one brotherhood, taught to live together and eat together in mutual love. They were also trained to defend themselves together against state repression. The social revolution started by Guru Nanak reached its goal. Those who hated each other, took *Amrit* **together from the same bowl and were commissioned as** *Sant Sipahi* **(Holy Soldiers) for serving society without distinction of caste, creed, or faith.**

To harass this new body, the Khalsa Panth, the rajas would think of one or another excuse to start an armed clash with them. More than half a dozen battles were forced on the Guru during his stay at Anandpur Sahib, a place purchased and developed by his father, Guru Tegh Bahadur.

In 1704, Anandpur Sahib was encircled by the joint forces of the Delhi emperor, the rajas and the governors of Lahore and Sirhind. Even this large army could not defeat the Guru. The siege continued for many months but to no avail. The Sikhs would come out of their forts, attack the army and carry the required rations inside. The financial burden of maintaining thousands of people required to lay siege to Anandpur Sahib put a great strain on the attacking Generals. In an effort to save face, they requested the Guru to move out of Anandpur Sahib voluntarily to preach his faith in other areas of the country. He was promised safe passage and permission to return to Anandpur Sahib later, if he so desired. By doing so, the aggressors thought they would then be able to claim 'victory' for having Anandpur vacated from the Guru.

As soon as the Sikhs came out of the forts, the forces could not resist the temptation to attack them. They wanted to claim an armed victory over them, forgetting all their solemn promises. The Guru, while defending himself moved on, crossed the Sirsa *nadi* (rivulet) and reached Chamkaur village. There he occupied a mud building which served as a *Garhi* or miniature fort. Fresh troops arrived to support the joint forces. The Guru had with him only forty men. They were exhausted and hungry. Even with such heavy odds against him, the Guru did not surrender. He killed one of the army generals with his arrow. Many other brave

43

men of the army were killed by the Sikhs who remained undefeated. The two older sons of the Guru, Ajit Singh (17 years), Jujhar Singh (14 years), and about thirty other Sikhs attained martyrdom fighting wave after wave of men sent to attack the fortress.

Having been successful in preventing the huge army's entry into the *Garhi,* the Sikhs decided upon their next strategy. Accordingly, the Guru left the mud building at midnight along with Bhai Maan Singh, Bhai Dharam Singh and Bhai Daya Singh, leaving the others to keep the Mughal army busy the next morning. To confuse the army commanders, the Guru put his *Kalghi,* ceremonial plume, on Sangat Singh, who looked like the Guru and was one of the Sikhs left behind. The next day, the Sikhs continued to fight to the last man. The army then celebrated their success for having killed the 'Guru', not knowing that he had already escaped through the kilometers of enemy camps spread around the mud house.

The mother of the Guru, along with the Guru's two younger sons, got separated from the Guru while the Sikhs were crossing the flooded Sirsa *nadi.* They were caught by the enemy and brought to Sirhind where the Nawab did his best to convert the two children to Islam. However, Baba Zorawar Singh (nine years) and Baba Fateh Singh (seven years) refused to succumb to his bribes and threats. The Nawab, therefore, had them killed by bricking them alive in a wall. The Nawab of Malerkotla questioned the killing of the innocent children and called it a great sin. He predicted that it would bring doom to the Nawab and his rule. This prophecy actually came to pass. About five years later, Banda Bahadur killed the Nawab and destroyed Sirhind. (See Chapter V). Because of his humane feelings, the Sikhs continue to show great regard for the Nawab of Malerkotla and his descendants till today.

(II) ZAFAR NAMAH

When the Mughals realized that the Guru had escaped, they immediately started on intense search for him that was to no avail. The Guru, along with the three Singhs, moved from one village to another to reach Alamgir (Ludhiana). After this, he went on horse back to Dina Kangar (Faridkot). There, he wrote the Zafar Namah, the letter of victory, to Aurangzeb. The Guru wrote to Aurangzeb that he was as cunning as a fox, and that his generals had broken all of the solemn promises made in the name of God. The Guru warned the emperor, "The Khalsa is alive and will remain so forever. The Khalsa will end your repression very soon." Aurangzeb repented and apologized for all the sins committed by him and his forces. He requested that the Guru meet him personally. He sent his emissary to guide the Guru to Aurangabad, a city in the South of India, where the emperor was forced to stay because of a serious illness.

THE WAR WON

Meanwhile, the Guru moved into the dry region of Bhatinda. The Mughal forces, still searching for him, finally met up with him at Mukatsar, then known as Khidrana Dhab (a small lake). They were defeated by the Guru in a bloody battle and forced to retreat, leaving their wounded unattended. Thus, the Guru humbled the mighty empire of Delhi and the Rajput rajas of the Himachal. The surviving Mughal soldiers returned to their headquarters feeling satisfied that they had been 'successful' in pushing the Guru out of Anandpur Sahib, far away to the dry region of Malwa. After this last battle, the Guru settled at Talwandi Sabo, now Damdama Sahib, District Bhatinda. Sikhs started coming to him from all over the Panjab and even distant states. Talwandi Sabo became an important seat of the Sikh faith, and as active a center as Anandpur Sahib. The Guru got prepared copies of Sri Guru Granth Sahib and sent these to major Sikh centers. A school of Sikh studies was started by Guru Gobind Singh at Talwandi Sabo.

Meanwhile, Aurangzeb's messenger carrying the response to the Zafar Namah reached Talwandi Sabo. The emperor, who was seriously sick, regretted the actions of his generals and invited the Guru to personally talk to him. As a result of which the Guru decided to undertake the journey to the south. Before the Guru had even gone half way, the emperor died repenting his sins. Aurangzeb's sons started to fight over the throne. The Guru agreed to help Bahadur Shah who was Aurangzeb's oldest son and his legal heir. By defeating his rivals, Bahadur Shah became the emperor of India. In recognition of the timely and critical help rendered by the Guru, Bahadur Shah honored him at a big reception in Agra. After this reconciliation, the Guru and the new emperor left for the south but parted at Nanded (Maharashtra) where the Guru stayed on the banks of the river Godawari. The emperor moved on but did not fulfill his promise to punish the guilty officials who had terrorized the Sikhs and killed the Guru's innocent young children. Therefore, the Guru deputed Banda Singh Bahadur to go to Panjab, and end the rule of the tyrants to bring peace to the state.

Before meeting the Guru, Banda was a *Bairagi Sadhu (recluse)*, who lived in a hut built in the forest near Nanded. While hunting, once the Guru happened to go to his hut. The *sadhu* was impressed by his holiness. When the Guru asked him who he was, the *sadhu* replied, "My Master, I am your Banda." Banda means a disciple who commits his life to his master. Later, the *sadhu* adopted Sikhism and was given a new name, Gurbakhsh Singh. However, he remained popular as Banda among the Sikhs.

A few weeks after the departure of Banda Singh Bahadur, the Guru was attacked when he was alone and about to go to bed. He was fatally wounded by the assassins deputed by the Nawab of Sirhind. The Nawab wanted to get the Guru killed before he (the Guru) could convince the Emperor to punish him (the Nawab) for his crimes. After some days the Guru died and was cremated there. Sikhs pay homage to the Guru at the Gurdwara built on that site, Abichal Nagar (Hazoor Sahib), Nanded, Maharashtra.

CHAPTER III

SRI GURU GRANTH SAHIB

The first compilation of Sri Granth Sahib included the Gurbani of the first five Gurus, hymns composed by fifteen *Bhagats* (devotees) and about a dozen other holy persons. It was compiled by Guru Arjun Dev in 1604 and was transcribed by Bhai Gurdas. Sri Granth Sahib was enthroned in the Harimandar Sahib in Amritsar. Pictures or paintings of the Gurus or any gods are conspicuous by their absence from the holy place. The final form of Sri Guru Granth Sahib was got prepared by Guru Gobind Singh; it was transcribed by Bhai Mani Singh. In this final version, the Gurbani composed by the ninth Nanak was included. Copies of this sacred compilation were sent to major Sikh centers in India.

Sri Guru Granth Sahib, in its first compilation was named *Pothi Sahib,* which means Sacred Scriptures. Gurbani was regarded and respected as the spirit of the Gurus. When Guru Gobind Singh, before his death at Nanded, formally invested the Guruship in the Gurbani, the name Sri Guru Granth Sahib became popular.

There is another compilation prepared many years after the demise of Guru Gobind Singh. It contains the hymns of Guru Gobind Singh and other writings based on Puranic mythology, particularly relating to Hindu Avtars including Rama and Krishna. The title "Guru" is given only to Sri Guru Granth Sahib and not to the Dasam Granth.

Sri Guru Granth Sahib contains some six thousand hymns. Major contributions are from the first and the fifth Gurus. Gurbani is grouped into thirty-one *Ragas.* Each *Raga* is classified into the *Chowpadey,* the *Ashtpadi,* and the *Chhand.* Within each of these sections, Gurbani is arranged in chronological order, so that the writings of the first Guru appear first, and so on.

In the beginning of Sri Guru Granth Sahib, preceding the Gurbani classified according to the *Ragas,* the Guru has incorporated three compositions : *Jap, Sodar,* and *Sohila* which form the preamble to the scripture. A Sikh should read *Jap* in the morning, *Sodar* in the evening, and *Sohila* before going to bed. The basic Sikh concepts of God are described in the *Mangla Charan*, the invocation, with which Gurbani in Sri Guru Granth Sahib begins. It is also written in abbreviated form or in full form, at the beginning of each *Raga*. It is repeated within the *Raga* where there is a change in the musical mode or where the author changes. *Var*, wherever present, forms the last part of the Gurbani in a *Raga*.

The *Bhagat Bani* or the hymns of the *Bhagats* follow the *Vars*. These *Bhagats include* Kabir, a weaver, Farid, a Muslim fakir, Nam Dev, a calico printer, Ravi Das, a shoemaker, Dhanna, an ordinary cultivator. Jaidev, Trilochan, RamaNand, Pipa, Sain, and Surdas are other *Bhagats* whose hymns are included in the scripture. The hymns of the *Bhagats* were incorporated into Sri Granth Sahib because they all speak of one God and the brotherhood of man. It is noteworthy that among these *Bhagats* are Muslims and Hindus of different classes including the so-called low castes, and even outcasts.

There are two other unique parts of Gurbani. The *Var* in Ramkali *Raga* is an account of the services of the first five gurus. It was written by Satta and Balwand, the two musicians of the Guru period. The other set of hymns, the Bhatt Bani, is written by a group of Bhatts, who were well educated and recognized as professional exponents of the Hindu scriptures. Bhatts visited Goindwal during the ministry of Guru Arjun Dev. They found in the Guru and the Gurbani, the peace and solace they had sought all their lives. These impressions are mentioned by them in their hymns.

At the very end of Sri Guru Granth Sahib, there are two concluding Shabads by Guru Arjun Dev. The first explains that the compilation contains *Amrit* Naam, the praise of the Lord. In the second hymn, the Guru thanks the Almighty for having got the sacred job of compiling Sri Granth Sahib done by him. The Guru prays to God for *Amrit* Naam.

Sri Guru Granth Sahib is written in Gurmukhi script. The language, which is most often *Sant Bhasha*, is very close to Panjabi. It is well undersood all over northern and northwest India and was popular among the wandering holy men. Many hymns contain words of different languages and dialects, depending upon the mother tongue of the writer or the language of the region where they were composed. Persian and some local dialects have also been used. Guru Nanak preached that no one particular language is more suitable than any other for praising God. A person can pray in any language and worship God by any name; essential component of the prayer is sincerity.

People who read, sing or listen regularly to Gurbani find such an occupation blissful. Gurbani explains the virtues of God, the Generator, Operator, and Destroyer of the universe. Gurbani contains no stories. It tells us the mission of human life, the ways to achieve it and to experience God. Some popular characters and mythological stories of Puranas and other old literature are cited as examples to explain that God is great and merciful.

MESSAGE OF SRI GURU GRANT SAHIB

Some of the important lessons, one learns by reading Gurbani, can be mentioned in brief as below.

(i) The invocation tells that God is the Lord of the whole universe. He alone is the Father-Mother for all of us. While the universe is moving and changing according to His Will, He alone is unchanged, beyond time; He is neither born and nor is He to die; He is ever self-existing. He loves His creation.

ੴ ਸਤਿ ਨਾਮੁ ਕਰਤਾ ਪੁਰਖੁ ਨਿਰਭਉ ਨਿਰਵੈਰੁ
ਅਕਾਲ ਮੂਰਤਿ ਅਜੂਨੀ ਸੈਭੰ ਗੁਰਪ੍ਰਸਾਦਿ ॥

(Guru Granth, p. 1)

(ii) All people are His children. No one community or people of any particular religion have a franchise on Him to claim that God is theirs alone and other communities will be sent to Hell.

ਤੂੰ ਸਾਝਾ ਸਾਹਿਬੁ ਬਾਪੁ ਹਮਾਰਾ ॥ (Guru Granth, p. 97)
ਆਪਨ ਬਾਪੈ ਨਾਹੀ ਕਿਸੀ ਕੋ ਭਾਵਨ ਕੋ ਹਰਿ ਰਾਜਾ ॥

(Guru Granth, p. 658)

(iii) All people will be judged by their deeds alone. Any one who loves God achieves the mission of human life.

We will be judged by our deeds and not by the name of the faith we adopt. There is only one religion; it is practiced not by performing rituals but by having sincere love for the people irrespective of their belief, caste, color, community, country, etc. Anyone who loves God can realize Him. Of course, we can address Him by innumerable names, Allah, Ram, Gobind, God, Guru, etc., depending upon one's liking and the community in which one is raised.

ਕਰਮੀ ਆਪੋ ਆਪਣੀ ਕੇ ਨੇੜੈ ਕੇ ਦੂਰਿ ॥

ਜਿਨੀ ਨਾਮੁ ਧਿਆਇਆ ਗਏ ਮਸਕਤਿ ਘਾਲਿ ॥

ਨਾਨਕ ਤੇ ਮੁਖ ਉਜਲੇ ਕੇਤੀ ਛੁਟੀ ਨਾਲਿ ॥ (Guru Granth, p. 8)

(iv) No person is a born sinner. Rather, this life has been gifted to us by God to enjoy singing His virtues. To love Him, one is to love all human beings, His children. Every person is His manifestation and every person has His reflection in him/her. The Gurbani says it in the following words :

ਭਈ ਪਰਾਪਤਿ ਮਾਨੁਖ ਦੇਹੁਰੀਆ ॥

ਗੋਬਿੰਦ ਮਿਲਣ ਕੀ ਇਹ ਤੇਰੀ ਬਰੀਆ ॥ (Guru Granth, p. 12)

ਸਭ ਮਹਿ ਜੋਤਿ ਜੋਤਿ ਹੈ ਸੋਇ ॥

ਤਿਸੁ ਦੈ ਚਾਨਣਿ ਸਭ ਮਹਿ ਚਾਨਣੁ ਹੋਇ ॥ (Guru Granth, p. 13)

(v) God Himself has created everything. He himself nurses them and destroys them as He wills. It is wrong to believe that there exists (or existed) any being other than God who can help or harm people according to his wishes. Gurbani tells us not to bother about *Satan*, Brahma, Vishnu, Mahesh, Inder; the poor fellows consider it to be lucky to have a chance to sing His praises standing at His door.

ਆਪੀਨੈ ਆਪੁ ਸਾਜਿਓ ਆਪੀਨੈ ਰਚਿਓ ਨਾਉ ॥

ਦੁਯੀ ਕੁਦਰਤਿ ਸਾਜੀਐ ਕਰਿ ਆਸਣੁ ਡਿਠੋ ਚਾਉ ॥

ਦਾਤਾ ਕਰਤਾ ਆਪਿ ਤੂੰ ਤੁਸਿ ਦੇਵਹਿ ਕਰਹਿ ਪਸਾਉ ॥

ਤੂੰ ਜਾਣੋਈ ਸਭਸੈ ਦੇ ਲੈਸਹਿ ਜਿੰਦੁ ਕਵਾਉ ॥

ਕਰਿ ਆਸਣੁ ਡਿਠੋ ਚਾਉ ॥ (Guru Granth, p. 463)

...ਗਾਵੈ ਰਾਜਾ ਧਰਮੁ ਦੁਆਰੇ ॥.....

ਗਾਵਹਿ ਈਸਰੁ ਬਰਮਾ ਦੇਵੀ ਸੋਹਨਿ ਸਦਾ ਸਵਾਰੇ ॥

(Guru Granth, p. 6)

(vi) The man-assumed Heaven and Hell are not particular places beyond our earth. When we love God and sing His virtues, we receive the blessings of God. It is living in Heaven. A person, who ignores to love God and suffers from ego, lust, anger, etc., lives actually in Hell on this very earth.

ਤਹਾ ਬੈਕੁੰਠ ਜਹਿ ਕੀਰਤਨੁ ਤੇਰਾ.....॥ (Guru Granth, p. 749)

ਕਬੀਰ ਆਸਾ ਕਰੀਐ ਰਾਮ ਕੀ ਅਵਰੈ ਆਸ ਨਿਰਾਸ ॥

ਨਰਕਿ ਪਰਹਿ ਤੇ ਮਾਨਈ ਜੋ ਹਰਿ ਨਾਮ ਉਦਾਸ ॥

(Guru Granth, p. 1369)

50

(vii) Gurbani says every day is a good day and very valuable in our life. A person is supposed to love God everyday and all the time. Every morning one should sit quietly to recite and concentrate on the virtues of God and do the same again when the day is over. Before going to bed, one is expected to tune one's mind to the blessings of God for a peaceful sleep and prepare for the day when he will 'sleep' for ever.

Some people believe a particular day to be sacred and more appropriate for prayers. They consider it a must to say their prayers on that day. Christians go to their church on Sunday while for Jews the sacred day is Saturday and for the Muslims it is Friday. Among the Hindus, certain days of the week are considered either auspicious or inauspicious; *Sankrant* (first day of the Indian solar month), *Pooran-masi* (full moon), and *Amavas* (no moon) days are considered sacred.

Gurbani rejects all these beliefs. It says God made days, not good or bad days. Those who worship days or dates, considering them to be auspicious or inauspicious, are native and ill informed.

ਸਤਿਗੁਰ ਬਾਝਹੁ ਅੰਧੁ ਗੁਬਾਰੁ ॥ ਥਿਤੀ ਵਾਰ ਸੇਵਹਿ ਮੁਗਧ ਗਵਾਰ ॥

(Guru Granth, p. 843)

UNIVERSAL FAITH

Sri Guru Granth Sahib is co-authored by persons born in more than one faith. It gives equal respect to all the different names of God mentioned by different religions and sects. It, therefore, proves the oneness of God. Many authors and philosophers have given their comments about the contents of Sri Guru Granth Sahib. All have noted the concept of universality preached by the Gurus and the *Bhagats* (devotees). The reader gets a logical and practical approach to the religion and realization of God.

To give an idea of what modern writers think about Sikhism and Gurbani, opinions of some famous authors are quoted below :

(i) Miss Pearl S. Buck, a Nobel laureate, while giving her comments on the English translation of Sri Guru Granth Sahib wrote[1] :

> *I have studied the scriptures of the great religions, but I do not find elsewhere the same power of appeal to the*

---

1. From the foreword to the English translation of Sri Guru Granth Sahib by Gopal Singh Dardi.

heart and mind as I find here in these volumes..... They speak to a person of any religion or of none. They speak for the human heart and the searching mind.

(ii) Rev. H. L. Bradshaw, of the USA, after thoroughly studying the philosophy of Sikhism, observed[1] :

Sikhism is a Universal world Faith, a message for all men. This is amply illustrated in the writings of the Gurus. Sikhs must cease to think of their faith as just another good religion and must begin to think in terms of Sikhism being the religion for this New Age....... The religion preached by Guru Nanak is the faith of the New Age. It completely supplants and fulfils all the former dispensations of older religions. Books must be written proving this. The other religions contain the truth, but Sikhism contains the fullness of truth.....

Bradshaw also says :

Sri Guru Granth Sahib of all the world religious scriptures, alone states that there are innumerable worlds and universes other than our own. The previous scriptures were all concerned only with this world and its spiritual counterpart. To imply that they spoke of other worlds as does Sri Guru Granth Sahib, is to stretch their obvious meanings out of context. The Sikh religion is truly the answer to the problems of the modern man.

(iii) Archer in his book on Sikh faith very rightly commented :

The religion of the Guru Granth is a universal and practical religion.....Due to ancient prejudices of the Sikhs it could not spread in the world. The world needs today its message of peace and love.

(iv) Another scholar Dorothy Field in her book, the Sikh Religion, writes :

Pure Sikhism is far above dependence on Hindu rituals and is capable of a distinct position as a world religion so long as Sikhs maintain their distinctiveness. The religion is also one which should appeal to the occidental mind. It is essentially a practical religion. If judged from the pragmatical standpoint which is a

---

1. Articles in the *Sikh Review,* Calcutta.

favorite point of view in some quarters, IT WOULD RANK ALMOST FIRST IN THE WORLD. (Emphasis by the author). Of no other religion can it be said that it has made a nation in so short a time.

Field further observed :

The religion of the Sikhs is one of the most interesting at present existing in India, possibly indeed in the whole world. A reading of the Granth strongly suggests that Sikhism should be regarded as a new and separate world religion rather than a reformed sect of Hinduism.

(v) Arnold Toynbee, a world famous British historian, writes[1] :

Mankind's religious future may be obscure; yet one thing can be foreseen. The living higher religions are going to influence each other more than ever before, in the days of increasing communications between all parts of the world and branches of human race. In this coming religious debate, the Sikh religion and its scriptures, the Guru Granth, will have something special of value to say to the rest of the world.

(vi) In his book, *The Sikh Religion*, Macauliffe writes :

Unlike the scriptures of other creeds, they do not contain love stories or accounts of wars waged for selfish considerations. They contain sublime truths, the study of which cannnot but elevate the reader spiritually, morally, and socially. There is not the least tinge of sectarianism in them. They teach the highest and purest principle that serve to bind man to man and inspire the believer with an ambition to serve his fellow men, to sacrifice all and die for their sake.

Macauliffe deems it necessary to draw the reader's attention to another significant feature of Sikhism, which distinguishes it and separates it from other philosophical and religious systems of thought :

The Sikh religion differs as regards the authenticity of its dogmas from most other great theological systems. Many of the great teachers the world has known, have not left a line of their own composition, and we only

---

1. Foreword to the Sacred Writings of the Sikhs by UNESCO.

know what they taught through tradition or second-band information. If Pythagoras wrote any of tenets, his writings have not descended to us. We know the teachings of Socrates only through the writings of Plato and Xenophon. Buddha has left no written memorials of his teaching. Kungfu-tze, known to Europeans as Confucious, left no documents in which he detailed the principles of his moral and social systems. The Founder of Christianity did not reduce his doctrines to writing, and for them we are obliged to trust to the Gospels according to Matthew, Mark, Luke, and John.

The Arabian Prophet did not himself reduce to writing the chapters of the Quran. They were written or compiled by his adherents and followers. But the compositions of the Sikh Gurus are preserved and we know first hand what they taught. They employed the vehicle of verse, which is generally unalterable by copyist, and we even become in time familiar with their different styles. No spurious compositions or extraneous dogmas, can therefore be represented as theirs.

The author of the *Vie de Jesus* was a great admirer of Jesus Christ. Greatly impressed as he was of the spiritual message delivered by Christ and those of the Semitic thinkers that preceded him, he posed the question : **"Whether great originality will again arise or the world be content to follow the paths opened by the daring creators of the ancient ages ?"** Having Sikhism in his mind, Macauliffe answers the above question in the following words :

Now there is here presented a religion totally unaffected by Semitic or Christian influences. Based on the concept of the unity of God, it rejected Hindu formalities and adopted an independent ethical system, ritual, and standards, which were totally opposed to the theological beliefs of Guru Nanak's age and country. As we shall see hereafter, it would be difficult to point to a religion of greater originality or to a more comprehensive ethical system.

Macauliffe tells us further :

Guru Nanak was not a priest either by birth or education, but a man who soared to the loftiest heights *of divine emotionalism, and **exalted his mental vision to an ethical ideal beyond the concept of Hinduism or Mohammedanism.***

The most numerous and powerful of all is the great Sikh sect (religion) founded by. Guru Nanak, which already forms a considerable section of the population of the Panjab, and which is scattered in greater or less numbers, not only throughout the whole of India but also in Kandhar, China and Southern Asia.

(vii) It will also be interesting to know the comments of Dr. W.O. Cole, of U.K. who has written more than half a dozen books on Sikhism. In 1985, he visited India where communal disturbances had created a virtual turmoil and thousands of people were killed. In a key note lecture[1] by him on the Mission and Message of Guru Nanak Dev, he gave a message to the *Sangat* there and through them to all of humanity : *Remember the tenets of Guru Nanak, his concepts of oneness of God and Universal Brotherhood of man. **If any community holds the key to national integration of India, it is the Sikhs all the way.***

After the lecture, he was asked what drew him to the study of Sikhism, he replied : *Theologically, I cannot answer the question what drew me to the study of Sikhism. You may call it, the purpose of God. But to be more specific, the unique concept of universality and the system of Langar (free community meal) in Sikhism are the two features that attract me towards the study of Sikhism. Langar is the exclusive feature of Sikhism and found nowhere else in the world. Sikhism is the only religion which welcomes each and everyone to its Langar without any discrimination of caste, creed, color or sex.*

(viii) The opinion of some Hindu mystics also needs to be quoted to know their experiences with the Sikh faith. Swami Nitya Nand (expired at the age of 135 years) writes in his book *Gur Gian* :

I, in the company of my guru, Brahma Nand Ji, went to Mathra......While on pilgrimage tour, we reached Panjab and there we met Swami Satya Nand Udasi. He explained the philosophy and religious practices of Nanak in such a way that Swami Brahma Nand Ji

---

1. Spokesman, Toronto, Canada.

enjoyed a mystic lore. During the visit to the Harimandar Sahib, Amritsar, his soul was so much affected, that he became a devotee of the Guru. After spending some time in Panjab he went to Hardwar. Though he was hail and hearty, one day I saw tears in his eyes. I asked the reason for that. He replied, "I sifted sand the whole of my life. The Truth was in the House of Nanak. I will have to take one more birth in that house, only then I will attain Kalyan." After saying that the soul left his body.

Swami Nitya Nand also wrote his own experience :

I also constantly meditate on Waheguru revealed by Nanak. I practiced Yoga Asanas under the guidance of Yogis and did that for many years; the bliss and peace, which I enjoy now, was never obtained earlier.

In other words, it is not only Sikhs who see that Sikhism, unlike most other religions, is a philosophy which has validity for all cultures but non-Sikh writers also strongly endorse this view.

(ix) In the end, it would be of great interest to mention here some glimpses from the proceedings of a seminar on the life of Guru Nanak Dev. It was conducted at Simla, now in Himachal Pardesh, by the Panjab Historical Society Lahore, before World War I, when the communal virus had not yet poisoned the minds of Indians. The seminar was presided over by the lieutenant governor of Panjab.

After hearing the lecture by Joginder Singh, Pundit Ramsaran Das, a prominent Hindu intellectual, observed that Guru Nanak was a great reformer of Hindu faith. Nawab Zulfikar Ali Khan of Malerkotla disagreed with Mr. Das and commented that Guru Nanak was a great Muslim fakir, his best friend was Bhai Mardana, a lowly Muslim. His best devotee was a Muslim, Rai Bhlar, the village chief. The governor, in his presidential remarks disagreed with both and said that according to what had been told by the speaker, Guru Nanak was a great Christian. The Guru, however, himself stated in Gurbani, "I am neither a Hindu nor a Muslim, I am a human being."

These are a few of the great number of comments given by literary and religious persons. Sikhs should take advantage of these observations of the non-Sikh writers. These opinions of world scholars and holy people should help Sikhs to develop greater devotion to their faith. Further, they should make Sikhs realize the need and importance of educating the youth about it.

THE SIKH CODE OF CONDUCT

Sikhism is a pious way of life for achieving peace by doing service to society. Some important principles of the Sikh faith for reaching that goal are described below :

(I) LOVING GOD (NAAM[1] JAPNA)

A Sikh is directed to concentrate his mind on God to reflect on God's virtues such as love, benevolence, and kindness. He practicies this to inculcate such virtues into his own character. This can be done by reciting Gurbani, by listening to the singing of hymns from Gurbani, or by sitting in a quiet place and attentively thinking of Him alone, forgetting everything else. Though constant meditation, a Sikh develops a feeling of affection and love for all humans, who are children of the same father, God. Such a person does not merely talk about the brotherhood of humanity but he actually tries to feel it all the time in his life. The thought of being a member of this human family becomes stronger and stronger and soon this fact is reflected in the daily behavior of the devotee. It gives him immense pleasure and satisfaction because he can observe the presence of God in every human being.

This achievement or realization changes the thinking and behavior of a person. Instead of hurting others, he enjoys utilizing his life serving needy persons. He cannot think of doing any act to harm a person, because he "observes" the living God inside every human being. This is why love of Naam is given the highest priority in the Sikh faith.

(II) HONEST LIVING (DHARM DI KIRT)

A Sikh is advised to earn his livelihood by the sweat of his brow. He is not supposed to be a parasite on society. A person who does not earn his livelihood may fall victim to hunger. An empty stomach may not make a person morally strong. When starving one is capable of trading off his religion, his morality, and his self-respect to fill his stomach. A non-earner becomes

---

1. Naam—it has a wide connotation. It refers to virtues of God and His authority managing the Universe.

dependent on others and because of his obligations, he is influenced to think and act as his bread-giver expects. Such a person cannot think or act independently.

A person's earnings, however large or small, should come from honest means. If a person is dishonest, and takes what is not justly his, these earnings are declared by the Gurus as the 'blood of the poor'. They are prohibited to a Sikh as beef is prohibited to a Hindu and pork to a Muslim.

There is always a great temptation to live a comfortable life by earning money through unfair means. The Guru wants us to resist this desire by keeping in mind that such earning pollutes the mind in the same way that blood stains our clothes. Only honest earnings are like "milk" and hence "sweet and tasty".

(III) SHARING WITH OTHERS (VAND KE CHHAKNA)

The recitation of Naam helps a person to realize that he is a member of the human brotherhood. This thought creates in him a feeling of kindness and love for those who need his help. As a consequence of it, he enjoys sharing his earnings with those who have not been as lucky as he is in meeting all their needs. Guru advises him that it is his duty to share his earnings with the needy, just as it is a duty of the parents to supply their children with clothing and other necessities.

This sharing must be done out of a sense of responsibility, and not of pride. A person can judge how near he is to God by sharing his bread with the needy. If he can do so without feeling proud that he has done someone a favor, then he is on the right path. Such acts provide one the feeling of true peace and happiness. Some people broadcast the fact that they are contributing to the needy and feel proud of their image as "benefactors". It is this pride (*ahankar*) which denies them the spiritual benefits obtained by a person who remains humble.

(IV) WORSHIPPING THE ETERNAL LORD (PUJA AKAL KI)

The Guru advises people to worship only the one almighty God. They should not concern themselves with the worshipping of the natural forces of the universe, or of any mythical powers which it is falsely hoped will mediate with God. It is the Creator not the creation that they should worship. Hinduism encourages its followers to venerate many different mediators. It differs from

Sikhism in this fundamental issue. Because of this difference Sikhism can in no way be considered a sect of Hinduism.

How does a Sikh worship God ? He does so by thinking of Him and by believing in the brotherhood of man. For Sikhs, God does not reside in the seventh or fourteenth sky, or any other place far from the earth. God lives in the hearts of humans. There is no place without Him. He expresses Himself through His creations. Worship of God in other terms means meditating on Him, His virtues and His grace.

(V) UNDERSTANDING GURBANI (PARCHA SABAD KA)

A Sikh should regularly read and understand Gurbani in Sri Guru Granth Sahib, which contains works by many authors of varied faiths and languages. Reading Gurbani teaches a Sikh what God's virtues are and how they can be revealed to him. Tales of ancient mythological incidents are used to illustrate God's message and His grace. The reader feels encouraged after knowing that many weak, poor, and even sinners realized God. One learns how the disciples became aware of His presence within them the moment they begin to love and serve humanity. The daily recitation of hymns reminds man repeatedly of the pitfalls such as egotism, lust, attachment, and greed, which can trap him. The hymns encourage the reader to develop good character by reminding him that these virtues bring peace to him and to his associates.

A Sikh accepts the word of the Guru as his guide. He regards Sri Guru Granth Sahib as his living Guru because he can obtain the spiritual guidance he needs, from Gurbani.

(VI) APPRECIATING THE SIKH REHT (DIDAR KHALSA KA)

A Sikh does not worship pictures or idols of God or the Guru. And neither does he honor any living individual as the Guru. Rather, he respects the decision of the corporate body of the Singhs, the Khalsa, since the tenth Guru bestowed the Guruship on this body. Even making of a picture or idol of the Guru is against the tenets of the Sikh faith.

(VII) WISHING WELL FOR HUMANITY (SARBAT KA BHALA)

The importance that Sikhs attach to working and wishing well for others can be seen in the fact that a Sikh prays aloud at least twice a day : "O God, in Your Name shower Your blessings on everyone." In other words, Sikhs pray not only for themselves alone but also for the whole brotherhood of humanity.

This belief in the oneness of humanity, and the insistence on working for the welfare of all people, whether Sikhs or not, at the cost of sacrificing one's life, is what sets Sikhism apart from other religions. In a world, which is torn by strife among different beliefs, Sikhism indeed shines brightly. Sikhs treat everyone with equal care and respect. All people, believers and non-believers, are offered free meals and other facilities in a gurdwara. A Sikh has no ill will against any person, including even their enemies. There are numerous examples of Sikhs helping an enemy in need. Bhai Kanahya, a water-carrier of the Guru at Anandpur Sahib, gave water and first aid to all wounded persons, Sikh and non-Sikh alike. It will be interesting for the Red Cross organizations to know that three centuries ago Guru Gobind Singh made arrangements to take care of and help all the wounded in a battle, whether his own men or his opponents.

It has been explained in the discussion of *Naam Japna* that Sikhs respect all persons. People may appear different because of their language, color, social habits but these variations are superficial and the result of different cultures and climates in which one is born and reared. Internally, we all have the same spirit. Just as gold can be made into ornaments of different designs but it remains gold, so people's outward appearances can be different but still they remain human beings created by the same God.

(VIII) MAINTAINING MORAL BEHAVIOUR (SACHA ACHAR)

For a Sikh, as for the followers of any other faith, lying, cheating, stealing etc. are forbidden. Sexual relations are restricted to married couples only. Recognizing that after a battle the women of the defeated side were often raped as an expression of power over the enemy, Guru Gobind Singh ordered that any person who raped a woman would be expelled from the Khalsa Panth.

The moral character of the Sikhs, in war and in peace, was praised highly by the Muslim historians of those times. Nur Mohammed, though express extreme hatred for Sikhs but he cannot help admitting their high character. He writes :

In no case would they slay a coward, nor would they

put an obstacle in the way of a fugitive. They do not plunder the wealth or ornaments of a woman, be she a well-to-do lady or a maid servant. There is no adultery among these 'dogs' nor are these mischievous people given to thieving. Whether a woman is young or old, they call her a 'buriya' and ask her to get out of the way. (The word "buriya" in the Indian language means an old lady.) *There is no thief at all among these 'dogs' nor is there any house-breaker born among these miscreants. They do not make friends with adulterers.*[1]

(IX) ACCEPTING THE WILL OF GOD (BHANA MANNANA)

Man suffers from the misconception that he alone is responsible for the benefits he gains from his labors. The fact is that these benefits are gifts from God. He is a mere actor on the stage. Rewards are given to us by God and whether or not our efforts are successful is according to His Will. If we accept this philosophy, we will always be in peace with ourselves and with our environment; we will stop worrying about the 'failure' of our efforts.

God had given us life, an expression of His Will. He has created the sun, the moon, vegetation, animals and everything else without which we cannot survive. When we plant a fruit tree, it grows natural, with the help of sun and rain, and it bears fruit all without our help. The smallest seed and the largest plant, are governed by laws of nature.

The philosophy, that everything happens according to God's will, can be explained by another example. A person driving on a road finds an old man walking. He stops the car, picks up the man, and drops him at his home. Although it appears that the driver's body has carried out these actions, but in fact, these actions originated in the mind because of a desire to help. Hence, actually it is the mind, controlled by the nature of the soul that helped the old man. The body of the driver was merely an agent, which executed the decision for the 'mind'. Similarly it is the bigger soul, God, who motivates us to act. We are the executors of His Will.

If we choose an action, which we think is right, only to discover that it does not eliminate the bad situation we set out to

---

1. Jang Nama as in Khushwant Singh's *A History of the Sikhs.*

abolish, we should not consider that our right action was useless. We should trust that in God's larger plan, which we cannot understand, our right action has meaning and effort. We must believe that every righteous action will eventually lead to a favorable result. The faith that our right actions are part of God's great design, even if we do not see the results, dispels worries about our failures and brings us peace and bliss. We will realize God's presence in ourselves. There is no higher goal in life than that.

(X) ABSTAINING FROM ADDICTIVE SUBSTANCES

Alcohol is prohibited for Sikhs, but some Sikhs do drink. To justify their action, they say, "Just a sip or two before dinner is not wrong. Drinking in excess and losing control of one's faculties, is, of course, bad and prohibited. A little drink is even recommended by doctors."

It is this thinking which has led many unwary persons to become alcoholics. Many addicts start from 'just tasting'. They had no intention of becoming alcoholics. An acquaintance of the author, on the author's consistent refusal to join him over a glass of whiskey, said, "*Sardar Ji*, if you have not touched it yet, never do. It is one of the most dangerous things in the world. This monster has eaten me up. I started with one glass just to overcome my fatigue and now I am the slave of this devil."

Many people begin to drink alcohol of use drugs, thinking that they will do so only in moderation, but discover too late, to their sorrow that they have become addicted. It is far easier to avoid these substances in the beginning than to wean one-self away from them later. Regarding drugs, including alcohol, it is always good to follow the maxim : *Be smart, don't start.*

Alcoholics and other addicts run a high risk of ruining their life and losing their jobs, thus creating great problems for many people beside themselves. Of course, some persons claim, "I have drunk alcohol for many years and have not become an alcoholic." But it is no guarantee that others can safely do so. Further, one might have become an alcoholic but one may not realize it during early stages. He will know it only when he gives it up. He may develop a craving for alcohol after a couple of months of giving it up and not within a few days or a couple of weeks.

It would be useful to give here some quotations from

Gurbani :

> *Alcohol is something to be detested. Even if it is prepared by using Gangajali (sacred water of the Ganges) saints do not consume alcohol, being a bad thing to drink.* (Guru Granth p. 1293)
> *One should "drink" the nectar of His Naam and not the useless alcohol. Drinking alcohol means losing the valuable life in gambling. A man absorbed in "drinking" (singing) His hymns is so much happier and filled with bliss that he does not bother even for the Heavens.*
> (Guru Granth p. 360)
> *If one wants to enjoy true ecstasy, he should "drink" the Naam of God, and that is the way to realize Him. One should strictly avoid alcohol by drinking of which one loses one's control of faculties. Alcoholics will be punished in His court.* (Guru Granth p. 554)

Just as cutting hair cannot really be blamed on the West neither can drinking alcohol be. Sikhs must take the responsibility themselves for their choices.

CHAPTER IV
FOUNDING OF THE KHALSA

In 1699 the tenth Nanak, Guru Gobind Rai, sent messages to his disciples all over the Indian subcontinent that he would have a special gathering at Anandpur Sahib on the day of Baisakhi. At this gathering, after the Gurbani recitation was over, the Guru drew his glittering sword and called for one brave Sikh to offer his head to save righteousness. Bhai Daya Ram of Lahore stood up and presented himself to the Guru. The Guru took him to a nearby tent and returned to the congregation shortly thereafter with a blood-demanding sword in his hand to ask for another head of a Sikh. This was repeated four times and four more Sikhs came forward to offer their heads to the Guru. They were Bhai Dharam Chand, a Jat of Delhi, Bhai Himat Das, a washer-man of Dwarka, Gujrat, Bhai Mohkam Chand, a calico pritner of Puri, Orissa, and Bhai Sahib Chand a barber of Bidar, Karnatka. Later, to the amazement of the whole congregation, all five Sikhs were brought back alive from the tent to the stage. They were dressed in special clothing.

The Guru prepared *Amrit*. It is water made sweet by adding sugar (*pattasas*) to it, and sanctified by reciting Gurbani while stirring it with a double-edged sword. These first five *Amritdhari* Sikhs, whom the Guru called "The Five Beloved Ones", were given the surnames "Singh". They were told that from then onwards they were no more Jats, Khatris, high or low castes. Everyone was equal and they were all like brothers. In this newly created brotherhood, the Khalsa, they were required to give up their caste names. Everyone after accepting *Amrit* became a Singh and the Singhs as a group were named the "Guru Khalsa Panth", now popular as simply Khalsa or Panth.

In order to become a Khalsa, one had to accept the 'Nash doctrine', the doctrine of destruction. It said that, for admittance to the Khalsa Panth a person had to give up his previous religion (*Dharam Nash*), rituals (*Karam Nash*) and also forget the caste (*Kul Nash*) assigned by the Brahmans. A person after becoming a Khalsa adopted a new faith, called Sikhism, a new surname,

Singh, and a code of conduct, the Khalsa Reht. The Khalsa got freedom from the meaningless hollow rituals forced on them by the Brahmans.

THE KHALSA CODE

(i) *Khalsa worships the Living Vibrant Spirit, Akal Purakh, (God) day and night and does not care for anyone else.*

ਜਾਗਤ ਜੋਤਿ ਜਪੈ ਨਿਸ ਬਾਸੁਰ ਏਕ ਬਿਨਾ ਮਨ ਨੈਕ ਨ ਆਨੈ ॥.....
ਪੂਰਨ ਜੋਤ ਜਗੈ ਘਟ ਮੈ ਤਬ ਖਾਲਸ ਤਾਹਿ ਨਖਾਲਸ ਜਾਨੈ ॥

(Guru Granth, p. 712)

(ii) *A Khalsa becomes a Saint Soldier of the Akal Purakh.*

ਖਾਲਸਾ ਅਕਾਲ ਪੁਰਖ ਕੀ ਫੌਜ ॥ ਪ੍ਰਗਟਿਓ ਖਾਲਸਾ ਪ੍ਰਮਾਤਮ ਕੀ ਮੌਜ ॥

(Sarabloh Granth)

(iii) *Everything of the Khalsa is a gift of God. Therefore, whatever belongs to him, including his body and mind, is at the disposal of the Guru. Obedience to the Guru is the path to God realization.*

ਤਨੁ ਮਨੁ ਧਨੁ ਸਭੁ ਸਉਪਿ ਗੁਰ ਕਉ ਹੁਕਮਿ ਮੰਨਿਐ ਪਾਈਐ ॥

(Guru Granth, p. 918)

The Khalsa were bestowed the full authority of the Guru to take decisions regarding the situation and problems faced by the Panth. The decisions, of course, were to be taken according to the directions of the Holy Granth. These decisions were to be respected and obeyed by all Sikhs as the orders of the Guru. A new community, which would not label a human being as low or high because of one's birth or wealth, was created. To join this community, the Guru himself requested the Five Beloved Ones to give *Amrit* to him. A unique practice had been inducted the Guru as "Singh" or a member of their corporate body. Thus, the Guruship passed to the Khalsa; Guru Gobind Rai was renamed Gobind Singh.

This was followed by mass induction of the disciples to the Khalsa Panth. Everyone who believed in the principles preached since Guru Nanak, was welcome to take *Amrit* and become a member of this new community. Different writers have given different figures regarding the number of Sikhs who took *Amrit* on that day. According to the intelligence reports sent to the emperor and subsequent writings of Sikh authors, it is said that more than 40,000 Sikhs took *Amrit* on this occasion. Taking

Amrit became a matter of great honor; any five *Amritdharis* had the authority to initiate other Sikhs and bring them into the Khalsa Panth.

The Persian term "Khalsa" was already in use those days. It meant the property of the emperor direclty under his jurisdiction. In Sikh writings, the term came into vogue during the time of Guru Har Gobind and it meant the Sikhs directly connected with the Guru.

Guru Amar Das established 22 preaching centers. Each Sikh center was managed by a nominee of the Guru. He was designated Masand. The Masands educated the *Sangat* regarding the Sikh faith, and collected their contributions to pass them to the Guru. When Guru Arjun Dev was tortured and martyred, some Masands did not remain sincere to the faith or loyal to the Guru. After the arrest of Guru Hargobind, more Masands became corrupt. They started extracting money from the Sikhs and misusing it for their pleasure. Therefore, later on, instead of nominating a Masand for the new disciples, the Guru adopted them himself and named them Khalsa. The Khalsa Sikhs made their offerings direct to the Guru and not through any Masand.

Guru Gobind Singh abolished the hereditary Masand institution because it had been deteriorating continuously. Some of the inheritors of this authority did not retain high character and devotion to faith expected of them. Some of them had even become corrupt. Main reason for their becoming corrupt was that the succeeding generations of the Masands got this status by inheritance and not by earning through their devotion to the faith.

Guru Gobind Singh used the term Khalsa for the *Amritdhari* Sikhs to signify that Khalsa Sikhs were the direct property of God, and not controlled by any gods. The Khalsa were honored as the Legions of the Lord of Eternity (*Akal Purkh ki Fauj*) and were required not to worship anyone but God, Who loves all people.

The Guruship of the Khalsa was thus ever-assured. No individual person was to be a Guru in the future. The corporate body would be the Guru and the decision of that body would be the decision of the Guru. Neither the Khalsa nor the Guru, could ever be destroyed. As long as humanity lives the Khalsa will remain alive. It can regenerate itself on the principles which were based on the brotherhood of human beings.

The founding of the Khalsa was the climax of the evolution of Sikhism. People, divided as Hindus and Muslims, or as low or high castes, were united into one brotherhood, and were taught :

(i) To live together with mutual love and affection.

(ii) To pray together as one body, the Sangat, addressing God by both Hindu names (Ram, Gobind, Krishan) and Muslim names (Allah, Kareem, Raheem), with equal affection. All these names were used for the One Almighty God, the Creator. Old sectarian names were thus given new meanings to create love among mutually hating people.

(iii) To eat together in Pangat along with other human beings regardless of their status, caste, belief or non-belief.

Thus, the religious and social revolution started by Guru Nanak reached its goal. The communities who hated each other were brought together into one brotherhood, the Khalsa.

MANDATE TO THE KHALSA

The purpose declared by the Guru for the founding of the Khalsa was briefly stated as below :

ਧਰਮ ਚਲਾਵਨ ਸੰਤ ਉਬਾਰਨ ॥ ਦੁਸਟ ਸਭਨ ਕੋ ਮੂਲ ਉਪਾਰਨ ॥
ਯਾਹੀ ਕਾਜ ਧਰਾ ਹਮ ਜਨਮੰ ॥ ਸਮਝ ਲੇਹੁ ਸਾਧੂ ਸਭ ਮਨਮੰ ॥

(Dasam Granth, p. 57)

- *To spread righteousness and to uproot the state repression and injustice.*

- *To end the evil of hatred for persons of low castes or other faiths and replace it with love for the whole of humanity, a family created by God.*

- *To inculcate self-confidence, to encourage people to live a humble (not weak) life of self-respect (not egotism) and to serve society as its honorable Sant Sipahi (holy policemen).*

The Khalsa were given a code of conduct for moral and religious living.

This code required that a Sikh should worship only one God, who was the Lord of not only the Sikhs but of all humanity. God can be worshipped by any name one may have for Him. A Sikh should recite Gurbani daily, in the early morning, in the evening and before going to bed. In addition to this, a Sikh is advised to visit a Gurdwara daily to benefit from the company of the Sangat, and enjoy *Kirtan*, the singing of divine hymns. A Sikh is not to worship any heavenly body such as the sun or moon. They are not permitted to worship images, pictures, or paintings of any god, not even of their own Gurus.

It should be noted here that the close association of Sikhs with Hindu culture has resulted in the adoption of many Hindu rituals by the Sikhs. Without realizing that they are contravening Sikh principles, many Sikhs have adopted prohibited practices. Pictorial representatives of the Gurus and their idols have been wrongly accepted by some Sikhs. They are even worshipped by a few Sikh in the same way as the Hindus worship their stone gods. This practice needs to be stopped immediately, otherwise Sikhism will lose its original spirit, foresight, and uniqueness. The Gurus never permitted paintings, busts, or sculptures of themselves to be prepared. They emphasized the philosophy of "Shabad Guru". Accordingly, Sri Guru Granth Sahib was enthroned in the Harimandar Sahib, Amritsar and it is the 'living' Guru for Sikhs. Whatever advice or religious instructions Sikhs need, they can find them in this sacred scripture.

Decisions concerning the *Sikh Reht Maryada,* the Sikh code of conduct, are the responsibility of the Guru Khalsa Panth, the corporate body of the Khalsa. They are to be respected and obeyed as edicts of the Guru would be. The Jathedar of the Akal Takht, the spokesman for this corporate body, meets with the representatives of the Khalsa to discuss the issues and announces the unanimous decisions taken by them. The decisions are always unanimous, because they are arrived at by a process of give and take, and based on Sikh philosophy and principles; it is not the opinion of the simple majority.

DO'S (REHT)

When the Guru initiated the Sikhs into the Khalsa, he simultaneously gave them the title of Sant-Sipahi (holy policemen). As is the case with every policeman in the world, a uniform was prescribed for them. It consists of five Ks : *Kesh,* uncut hair; Kirpan (a sword); *Kachha,* a particular style of underwear; *Kara,* an iron bangle; and *Kangha,* a comb.

The five K's are the gifts of love and pride to the Sikhs from the Guru. The uniform of a soldier or a policeman is the means by which the wearer identifies himself; a Sikh adopts the five

K's for much the same reason. They are a visible reminder of his commitment to the Sikh code of conduct. The Sikhs wear these five articles of their faith reminding them of the honor of being a Singh. Some authors have mistakenly tried to associate material benefits to the body as a reason for wearing the five K's. Such attempts undermine the true significance of the five K's, the articles of Sikh faith.

Uncut hair is compared to a lion's mane and said to make a person as brave as a lion. The story of hero Samson, who could not be defeated as long as his hair was uncut, is quoted as a proof that uncut hair give strength. The practice of keeping the hair uncut is further justified by stating that many prophets such as Christ, Mohammed, Ram and Krishan, had uncut hair. However, the Sikhs do not keep Kesh because of the example of the prophets or just because of their benefits to the body. It is the order of the Guru and the identity provided by the Kesh which are important. If the 18th century Sikhs insisted on uncut hair because of its physical benefits, they could hardly choose death in preference to cutting their hair. Hair are kept uncut for religious reasons and nor for reasons of physical benefit to the body. Any person, who voluntarily agrees to be a visible Sikh, has to wear the five K's to express his/her commitment to Sikhism, irrespective of their physical benefits or problems to him/her.

DON'TS (KUREHT)

Four actions are forbidden to the Sikhs. A person loses his membership in the Khalsa and can no more claim to be a Singh if he or she (i) cuts hair from any part of his/her body, (ii) engages in sexual activity with a person other than the spouse, (iii) uses drugs, tobacco, alcohol, etc. or (iv) consumes *Halal*, meat butchered by performing Muslim religious rites.

Anyone who commits one or more of these four prohibited acts, must present himself for retaking *Amrit* and explain the reasons for having strayed away from the prescribed Khalsa discipline. After retaking *Amrit*, and performing duties given to him/her (*Tankhah*) the Sikh becomes an equal member of the Khalsa again.[1]

---

1. A copy of the Sikh Reht Maryada is available free, from every Gurdwara. Every Sikh is expected to read it carefully in order to understand Sikh practices as well as Gurdwara protocol.

UNIQUENESS OF THE SIKH FAITH

Sikhism is not a combination of good principles selected from Islam and Hinduism. However, many non-Sikhs and even some Sikhs have **wrongly concluded** that Sikhism was founded by combining the rational and acceptable beliefs of Islam and Hinduism. According to them, the first Nanak created the Sikh religion by choosing several ideas from the Hindu faith such as the *Karma* theory. It says whatever we get in this life is the fruit of our *Karam* or deeds in our previous life and whatever we do in this life will bear fruit in the next life. He accepted the Muslim belief of one God, the only Supreme power. Guru Nanak excluded from Sikhism the bigotry of the Muslims and their philosophy of forcible conversions. He also excluded several Hindu practices, such as the worshipping of many different gods and their idols.

Actually, Guru Nanak revealed several unique ideas, which have nothing to do with Hinduism or Islam. It is important to understand the basic Sikh concepts, which set Sikhism distinct from other religions.

Guru Nanak's view is that God is not sectarian. The Guru disagreed with the Muslim belief that God, Allah, because of the intercession of the prophet Mohammed, would welcome only Muslims into *Bahisht* (Heaven) and throw *Kafirs* (non-Muslims) into the fire of *Dozakh* (Hell). In the same way, he disagreed with the Hindu idea that God, Bhagwan, would admit only high caste Hindus to Heaven and throw Muslims and others into Hell. Furthermore, the Guru rejected the idea that there were many gods, all of whom must be wooed with gifts of food and sacrifices of animals or humans.

Guru Nanak preached a new definition of God and His relationship with humanity. *All people are equal and are loved by the Father, God. Anybody who loves Him by any name realizes Him.*

ਜਿਨੀ ਨਾਮੁ ਧਿਆਇਆ ਗਏ ਮਸਕਤਿ ਘਾਲਿ ॥
ਨਾਨਕ ਤੇ ਮੁਖ ਉਜਲੇ ਕੇਤੀ ਛੁਟੀ ਨਾਲਿ ॥

(Guru Granth, p. 8)

He, thus, founded a sovereign faith independent of the existing faiths.

Guru Nanak criticized the Hindu *Karma* theory. He observed, "If we believe that what we do here in this life is the result of

70

our actions in the previous birth, then on what basis did we perform our actions in our first life when we joined the cycle of births and deaths? How could a soul enter the first life of its cycle, if the only criterion is the soul's actions in its previous life ? A soul entering its first life would have no past actions on which to base its entrance."

Guru Nanak taught that a person who sincerely repented of a misdeed, and thus became aware of the true meaning of life, thereby redeemed himself. A person, who does not repent and closes his mind to truth and justice, removes himself further from the awareness of God. He will have to pass through more lives to achieve that awareness.

Just as Sikhism's interpretation of *Karma* theory is different from that of Hinduism, so are Sikhism's reasons for cremating the dead different from those of Hinduism. Sikhism does not restrict the way in which a dead body may be disposed. People may bury the body, throw it in water, cremate it, or treat it in any convenient but respectful way. None of these methods helps or harms the soul in any way. The soul is not affected by any physical treatment to the body. For Sikhs, the cremation is a convenient way of disposing of a dead body. In contrast, cremation of the dead body according to Hinduism is a religious act while Christians and Muslims believe that the body should be buried and not cremated.

In the end, it may be concluded that one of the great strengths of Sikhism is its universal appeal. It works for the good of all people regardless of their religion and has, as its nucleus, not a collection of rituals and dogmas, but a belief in the search of truth and justice. For this reason scholars, who have studied Sikhism, call it the religion of the modern man. (See Chapter III for the opinions of the scholars)

CHAPTER V
THE GURU KHALSA PANTH

The *Sangat,* instituted by Guru Nanak, was given the status of the Guru Khalsa Panth by Guru Gobind Singh as already mentioned in Chapter IV. Every person, high caste or low caste, rich or poor, Hindu or Muslim, who believed in Sikhism and who was willing to follow the sublime path of the faith, was welcome to become a member of the Khalsa.

After the death of the Guru in 1708 at Nanded, the period of Guruship by an individual person ended. All political and social decisions after that were to be taken by the Guru Khalsa, the corporate body of the Singhs. According to the Khalsa principles, each member in his own right is a disciple of the Guru and believes that the Guru is always with him as long as he tries to act correctly. When consulted, each member gives his considered opinion. Then all suggestions are weighed objectively and a consensus is reached. The joint decision of the Khalsa is considered an order of the Guru and it is honored by every Sikh, whatever his original opinion might have been. The Akal Takht is the seat where these decisions are made.

The 18th century history of the Guru Khalsa Panth provides a glorious inspiration for the Sikhs. The supreme and unparalleled sacrifices during this period made by the Khalsa to end state repression against innocent citizens are recited in the Ardas. The Sikhs lived either in the dry areas of the south west of Panjab or in the thick forests of the northern Panjab or other inhospitable places. There they could obtain some respite from the persecution by the State army and the local police, both of which had orders to kill every Sikh on sight. Even the Muslim historians of the time, who were writing from the point of view of the Sikh persecutors, praise the character and bravery of the Sikhs. This era is known as the Golden Period of Sikh history.

The Muslim rulers declared a war against the Sikhs because only the Sikhs were making concerted efforts to resist the State policy of forcible conversion and repression of human rights. One name from this period which Sikhs honor greatly is that of

Baba Banda Singh Bahadur. Guru Gobind Singh, just before his death in 1708, deputed him to go to Panjab and to help people suffering under the tyranny of the Mughal rule. He was assisted by five Singhs including Bhai Baj Singh.

They arrived in the Panjab with a handful of Sikhs in the winter of 1709. The most powerful and valuable 'arm' he brought with him was a Hukamnama, an edict, from Guru Gobind Singh. It desired the Sikhs to join Banda and wage a war to finish the tyrant rulers. This edict very strongly charged the minds of the people weary of the oppressive government.

Banda was welcomed in Panjab and a large number of Sikhs offered to serve the cause of the Khalsa. Banda had to fight only minor battles to gain control of Panipat, Samana, Sadhora, and several other places. Soon he was in a position to challenge the Nawab of Sirhind, about two hundred and fifty kilometers from Delhi. The successes of the Khalsa were so spectacular that many believed they were only possible because Banda had some mysterious powers under his control which helped him to win battles so easily. Actually, this mysterious power was the support of the masses, who perceived Banda as their savior. Glorious victories of the Sikhs under the command of Banda were seen as the beginning of the end of the Mughal rule in India. Later, it proved to be true.

The Mughal army, though much larger and better equipped than Banda's, could not stand against Sikhs fighting on the strength of their principles. The Nawab was killed and Sirhind was destroyed. Nearby there was a Muslim holy place, Sirhind Sharif, the burial spot of Sheikh Ahmed Sirhindi. Sheikh had hatched the conspiracy to kill Guru Arjun Dev with the support of the then emperor, Jahangir. The Khalsa, true to its principles, respected the sanctity of this place and did not vandalize it or damage it. In contrast the Mughals often destroyed the Sikh holy places in their attempts to annihilate Sikhs.

Shaken by this success of the Khalsa, the emperor in Delhi issued orders in December 1710, that a Sikh, wherever he was seen, should be killed.

Emperor Bahadur Shah himself organized all his forces to arrest or kill Banda. He withdrew his army from all other campaigns and recruited mercenaries for this mission. However, Shah was disappointed when he found that Banda had slipped into the hilly areas and had gone beyond his reach. His failure to catch Banda gave him a severe shock, and as a result he became mentally sick and soon died. He was succeeded by Farkh Syer.

When in 1715 Banda again took over some parts of northern Panjab, a very strong army was deputed to either catch or kill him at any cost. Banda took refuge in a small village, Gurdas Nangal, near Gurdaspur.

Starving and surrounded by the army, Banda and his men fought bravely. An eyewitness, Mohd Qasim[1] gave the following account of the siege :

The brave and daring deeds of the infernal Sikhs were amazing. Twice or thrice every day some forty or fifty of these black-faced infidels came out of their enclosure to gather grass for their cattle and when the combined forces of the imperialists went to oppose them, they made an end of the Mughals with arrows, muskets, and small swords and disappeared. Such was the terror of the Sikhs and the fear of the sorceries of the Sikh chief that the commanders of the army prayed that God might so ordain things that Banda should seek safety in his flight from the fortrees.

The army failed to capture Banda, therefore they tried a trick. Under the pretense of arranging a settlement between Banda and the emperor, they persuaded Banda to agree to a discussion. The governor of Lahore promised Banda the rule of Jammu and the adjoining hill areas in return for Banda's reconciliation with the Delhi administration. However, while the governor made a show of discussing terms with Banda, they captured him along with seven hundred men. They were taken to Delhi under strong guard. Their journey is described by Mohd Harisi, an eyewitness, in the following words :

Those unfortunate Sikhs who had been reduced to this last extremity, were quite happy and contented with their fate; not the slightest sign of dejection or humiliation was to be seen on their faces. In fact most of them, as they passed along on their camels seemed happy and cheerful, joyfully singing the sacred hymns of their Scriptures.

---

1. *A History of the Sikhs*, Khushwant Singh, pp. 114-117.

Upon their arrival in Delhi, one hundred of them were murdered each day. None gave up his Sikh faith and each accepted death gladly. According[1] to a letter dated March 18, 1716 from the British representative in the Mughal court Delhi (an eyewitness to the massacre), to his Chief in Calcutta, the cold-blooded murder of the Sikhs started on March 5, 1716. About one hundred Sikhs were murdered every day in the space now attached to the Hardinge Library near Fountain, in Chandni Chowk. Everyone tried to be ahead of the other and argued for his priority for execution. It is not a little remarkable with what patience they undergo their fate and to the last it has not been found that one apostatized from this new formed religion.

The Muslim historian Khafi Khan who also observed this massacre, noted that **even a boy still in his teens refused to accept pardon by disclaiming his faith, but offered his head to the sword. His mother appealed to the emperor that her son should be set free because he was not a Sikh. The boy replied that his mother was a liar and claimed that he was indeed a Sikh and must be martyred the same way as his associates.** These blood-curdling murders of 1716 did not demoralize the Sikhs but made them more fearless and more determined to die for their faith rather than relinquish it.

The Delhi order of 1710, that Sikhs should be killed wherever seen, was issued again in 1716 and implemented even more vigorously and ruthlessly. In order to retain their beards and turbans, Sikhs retreated into the forests, deserts, and inhospitable places along riverbeds densely overgrown with sedge and bush. For fifty years Sikhs suffered inhuman tortures, the extent of which cannot be fully described by pen. Roving bands of the Mughal army spread over the countryside hunting for Sikhs. A reward was given to anyone who killed a Sikh, or who provided information leading to the capture or death of a Sikh. To be a Sikh meant to risk death for all of one's family. The sacrifices made by the Sikhs are now recalled daily in the Sikh prayer :

> *Let us remember and respect the holy sacrifices made by*
> *those who offered themselves for martyrdom; who were*
> *cut to pieces; who preferred to have their skulls sliced*

---

1. *The Sikh Review,* Calcutta, August 1988, p. 24.

*open rather than allow their hair to be cut; who were
sawed alive into two pieces; who were crushed between
rotating spiked wheels; who as mothers, watched their
children cut into pieces and wore the pieces as necklaces
around in their necks, remaining hungry, suffering
indescribable tortures but uttered not a word of pain;
who bore all this gladly, keeping to their faith,
maintaining their beloved symbols and their uncut hair
as long as there was breath in their body and uttering
God's Name no matter what was done to them. Hail the
Lord, Almighty!*

A brief description of Sikh life during this period, the Sikhs,
daring deeds and sacrifices, is given below :

MARTYRDOM OF BHAI MANI SINGH

After the execution of Banda Singh Bahadur, the Sikhs started
meeting at Amritsar twice a year, Baisakhi and Diwali. This
gathering was called Sarbat (all combined) Khalsa. They made
their decisions jointly after discussion and goodwill. Their
decisions were accepted by every Sikh and respected as orders of
the Guru. No member of the Khalsa, no matter how highly placed
he might be, ever thought of ignoring them.

Unfortunately, some differences regarding the interpretation
of the Sikh Reht split the Sikhs into two camps, the Tatt Khalsa
and the Bandai Khalsa. The later adopted amendments considered
to have been decided by Banda Bahadur and the former did not
agree with those. In 1721, Mata Sundri Ji, widow of Guru Gobind
Singh, stepped in and nominated Bhai Mani Singh, a holy man,
as the Granthi Sahib of Amritsar. Bhai Mani Singh discussed the
issue with both sides and the Sikhs amicably agreed to accept the
Tatt Khalsa as their leaders. The Khalsa, having united, emerged
as a strong power to be reckoned by the government. Some units
of the Khalsa took over a couple of villages near their hideouts.
The governor tried to bring them again under his control, but met
with failure, losing his men and his image.

The rulers decided that since the Sikhs had proved themselves
too strong and determined to be annihilated, they should be
befriended. A Nawabship and the revenues of a *Jagir* (a unit of
villages) were offered to the Khalsa on the condition that they
would not challenge the authority of the rulers. The Khalsa agreed

to co-operate and accepted the offer in the name of Sardar Kapur Singh, who became known as Nawab Kapur Singh. He, helped by the other great Sikh leader, Jassa Singh Ahluwalia, took full advantage of this period of truce. All *Jathas* (independent units of the Khalsa) were merged together and named Dal Khalsa. They were grouped into two forces, Budha Dal, the experienced elder Sikhs, and Taruna Dal, the young fighting Sikhs, usually under 35 years. The Khalsa, thus organized, took more areas under their control.

The increasing strength of the Khalsa was not to the liking of the governor, Zakria Khan. He confiscated the *Jagir granted a few years earlier,* and he himself guided the army to push the Sikhs out of Panjab. Dal Khalsa was obliged to leave Amritsar and cross the two rivers Beas and Sutlej to take refuge in the dry tracts of Malwa.

In 1738, Bhai Mani Singh approached the government for permission to have a general gathering of the Sikhs on the day of Diwali. They agreed to it if he paid a tax of 5000 rupees. Accordingly messages were sent to the Sikhs hiding in far off places to visit Amritsar. When Diwali approached, the arrival of the army around Amritsar created doubts in the minds of the Sikhs regarding the sincerity of the government. A revised message was sent to the Sikhs not to visit Amritsar lest they be caught in the army net. The governor, captured Bhai Mani Singh, and ordered him to pay the money or become a Muslim. Bhai Sahib argued that the government broke their promise by sending their army to Amritsar. As they did not permit free gathering of the Khalsa, no money was due to them. Upon his refusal to pay the money to the government or convert to Islam, Bhai Mani Singh was tortured and hacked to pieces joint by joint. The Khalsa were enraged by the murder of their holy, beloved and respected priest. They intensified their efforts to get rid of the tyrant rulers.

HUNTING AND TORTURE OF THE SIKHS

The Mughal ruler decided to prevent Sikhs from visiting the Harimandar Sahib in Amritsar, their source of life and spirit. The army guarded the Harimandar Sahib so that no Sikh could come to bathe in the *Sarovar* and pay homage to his Guru. The Sikhs, in their prayer, begged the Lord to bestow upon them *'Amritsar De Darshan Ishnan'*– a visit to Amritsar and a bath in the *Sarovar.*

These words since then have become a part of their daily prayer to commemorate this part of Sikh history. The Sikhs continued to risk their lives in order to fulfil the satisfaction of a bath in the *Sarovar*. Those caught on their way to the *Amrit Sarovar* suffered torture and death. According to some eyewitness Muslim historians, none of those caught could be induced to give up their faith in order to survive.

During this very time, Nadir Shah from Persia, invaded India. Zakria surrendered himself to Nadir without any resistance. Nadir, therefore, proceeded to take over Delhi. He looted the capital and took possession of the Kohi-Noor, the world's largest diamond.[1] He made thousands of people his slaves, and ordered them to march to his home country. While he was returning through Panjab, the Dal Khalsa lightened much of his load and freed many of the prisoners. The Khalsa would come like hawks, do their job, and ride away before the army guards knew what had happened.

By this, the Khalsa not only obtained much-needed funds, but retrieved the honor of the country, thereby winning a moral battle against the governor. The people accepted the brave Sikhs as their saviors who risked death to free the prisoners from the invader while the governor had sheepishly submitted. Khalsa also became confident of their ability to defeat the rulers and to be the master of their own state.

Nadir Shah, impatient with this Sikh harassment asked Zakria Khan, the governor of Lahore in 1739, "Who are these men with turbans and beards ? Where do they live ? Why can't you finish them once and for all ?" The governor replied, "They are fakirs and have no houses; they live on horseback and camp in the forests." After hearing this, Nadir Shah rightly observed, "I smell in them the power to rule. Keep an eye on them."

Efforts to put down the Sikhs were, therefore, further intensified. Zakria ordered village officials all over the state to hunt down the Sikhs, catch them, or kill them.He put a graded price on them. One could get money by killing a Sikh, cutting off the hair of a Sikh, disclosing their hideouts, or providing

---

1. Later, the Sikhs recovered the Kohi-Noor during the time of Maharaja Ranjit Singh. Since 1849, when the British took over Panjab, the diamond is with the monarch of the United Kingdom.

information leading to their arrest. Police stations would hand out money in exchange for the head of a Sikh. Cartloads of severed Sikh heads were sent to Lahore as proof of their achievement by the local authorities.

The Sikhs who were arrested alive were taken to Lahore in chains. They were starved and tortured. Finally, they were butchered before the eyes of big gatherings in the horse market at a place later named Shaheed Ganj, A Gurdwara now stands there in memory of those martyrs.

In 1740, the Amritsar *Sarovar* was filled with debris and a local chief, a Rangarh named Massa, was put in charge of it by the government. He used to sit and smoke there, watching half-naked nautch girls perform in the Harimandar Sahib. When the Sikhs camping in Bikaner, a desert area of Rajasthan, learned of this desecration, they were furious. Two of them, Bhai Sukha Singh and Bhai Mehtab Singh, decided to put a stop to it. They travelled to Amritsar, and went to the Harimandar Sahib disguised as revenue officials. One of them approached Massa, drew his sword and suddenly beheaded him. The other Sikh quickly picked up the head and both of them rode off on their horses before the dancing girls could overcome their shock and alert the guards.

THE FIRST SIKH HOLOCAUST

Zakria died in 1745. The Sikhs felt some relief. They advised villagers to rid themselves of the Mughal tyrant rule. This enraged the government. The minister, Lakhpat Rai, sent his brother, Jaspat Rai, to control the Sikhs, but he was killed in a battle. For his safety Jaspat was riding an elephant during a fight with the Sikhs. A smart Sikh suddenly caught the tail of the elephant, climbed on his back and chopped off the head of Jaspat.

Angered by this, the Mughals instructed their army to seek out the Sikhs and kill them. Sikhs in Lahore were arrested, brought to Shaheed Ganj and executed. Copies of Sri Guru Granth Sahib were located and burnt. The Khalsa decided to move away towards the hills for safety. But they were pursued amidst the sedges and reefs along the Beas river in the Kahnuwan area of the district of Gurdaspur. The local people were forced to join the army to search for Sikhs and kill them. About then thousand of them were massacred there in what became known as the Chhota Ghalughara (small holocaust). This devastating blow to the Sikhs

79

in 1746 made them more determined than ever before to put an end to the genocide.

Up until then, the Sikhs were grouped into small *Jathas* which functioned usually independently of each other. In April 1748, at the Akal Takht in Amritsar, Nawab Kapur Singh organized the Dal Khalsa into five divisions or Misls. Jassa Singh Ahluwalia had the overall command. Later, their number increased to eleven. The 12th Misl of Phulkian, which ruled Malwa region, was not the composite part of the Dal Khalsa. One of the Misls' first decisions was to agree that Panjab belonged to Sikhs and that they would defend it with their might.

In 1748, Mir Mannu became the governor of Panjab. At first, he refrained from unnecessarily incurring the wrath of the Sikhs. Minister Kaura Mal played a good role in this.

Ahmed Shah Abdali, the king of Afghanistan was a yearly menance for the Panjab and Delhi. However Mir Mannu received no help from Delhi to fight Abdali and defend Panjab. He, therefore, changed his loyalties after 1751. He allied himself with Ahmed Shah Abdali, instead of with the emperor of Delhi. Abdali advised Mir Mannu to repress the Sikhs. Hence, hunting of the Sikhs started again all over Panjab. If the males escaped arrest, the females were brought to Lahore to be tortured and butchered. Shaheed Ganj Gurdwara stands in Lahore in the memory of these Sikhs. The women were imprisoned, starved and forced to work in labor camps. Their children were chopped into pieces and strung around their necks as necklaces. To boost their morale the Sikhs chanted :

We, the plants, and Mannu, the sickle, all know.
The more he cuts us, the more we grow.

The Sikhs refused to submit to Mannu's tyranny. Mannu died in 1753 and the Panjab was again in the hands of the Khalsa. They parceled the state among the Misls and became its *de facto* rulers.

MARTYRDOM OF BABA DEEP SINGH

In 1756, Abdali attacked Delhi for the fourth time and defeated the Mughal government. He looted the whole of North India including Delhi, Mathra and Agra. While he was returning with a caravan loaded with gold and valuables along with thousands of men and women prisoners, the Sikhs attacked him.

The prisoners were freed and escorted to their homes and most of the treasure was also taken away from him. Ahmed Shah was stunned by his defeat at the hands of the 'brigands', the name he used for the Sikhs.

In anger, he desecrated the Harimandar Sahib and filled the *Sarovar* with debris. He deployed ten thousand Afghan soldiers under the command of General Jahan Khan to destroy the Sikhs. He made his son Temur, the governor of Panjab.

Baba Deep Singh, who was at Damdama Sahib near Bhatinda, set out for Amritsar with a few thousand men, as soon as he learned of this desecration. The Sikhs vowed either to liberate the city and rebuild the temple or die in the service of the Guru. They fought bravely against the well supplied and well-equipped army occupying the city. Jahan Khan ordered all able-bodied men to join him to check the advance of the Sikhs. Fighting columns of the determined Sikhs led by Baba Ji., however, did reach the Harimandar Sahib. Baba Deep Singh was one of many who gave up his life for Sikh principles and became a martyr.

The martyrdom of Baba Deep Singh and his associates shocked the whole Sikh nation. They determined to retaliate with vengeance. Jathedar Jassa Singh sent for all Sardars to join him. Adina Beg, the Faujdar of Jalandhar, had not submitted his dues to Lahore. He also wanted to weaken the governor so that he could remain master of the Jalandhar Doab. Beg therefore supported the Sikhs. The Sikhs defeated the Afghan army near Hoshiarpur. After this crushing defeat, Temur made many attempts to project the image of being the governor but it was the Sikh writ which ruled everywhere. The Afghanas suffered one defeat after another and would not dare to come out of Lahore and face the Sikhs. The Sikhs became virtual rulers of the Panjab. They collected the *Rakhi* (revenue) from most of the areas in the state. Even Adina Beg agreed to pay *Rakhi* to the Sikhs for protecting Jalandhar.

Adina Beg was tempted to take advantage of weak Temur and become the governor himself. He asked the Marhattas to help him. Being certain they would not be able to protect themselves from the joint forces of the Sikhs and the Marhattas, Temur and Jahan Khan vacated Lahore. While retreating to their country, some of the Afghans and their guns were intercepted by the Sikhs near the Chenab river. The Afghans were brought to Amritsar as prisoners and made to undo what they had done some months earlier in desecrating the *Amrit Sarovar.* **After the Afghans had cleaned the *Sarovar* and removed all the debris, they were freed without any other punishment. Historians have a lot of praise for the Sikh character. They say Sikhs never tortured or murdered their prisoners. This was unlike Mughals and Afghans, who always persecuted and publicly murdered Sikh captives, not even sparing innocent women and children.**

The Misls extended their *Rakhi* system over more areas of the Panjab. Their numbers also increased greatly after these successes.

THE SECOND SIKH HOLOCAUST

Abdali invaded India again in early 1761 when the famous battle of Panipat took place between him and the Marhattas. There were very heavy losses on both sides. Thousands of soldiers died. The Sikhs remained aloof and let both of the claimants to Panjab wear themselves out, leaving the Sikhs to be the masters of their lands.

Abdali won the battle and ravaged Delhi after his victory. When returning, the exhausted Afghan soldiers loaded with booty, found it impossible to withstand the lightning attack of the swift Sikhs. They appeared from nowhere, attacked the guards like hawks, took away the looted wealth, and vanished as quickly as they had come. The Khalsa not only liberated some 2000 women prisoners, but also took away much of the treasures, which Abdali had obtained from Delhi. Harassed and bothered by the Sikhs, he left Panjab dejected and extremely angered. After suffering severe damages and heavy losses of men at the hands of the Marhattas, he was returning empty handed to his country. Before leaving Panjab, he resolved in his mind to come back with enough force to destroy the Sikhs from the face of the earth.

In 1761, after Diwali, the Sikhs occupied Lahore. Jassa Singh Ahluwalia was given the title of Sultanul Kaum, or the King of the Sikh nation.

Abdali returned with a large organized force in February 1762. Knowing this, the Sikhs vacated Lahore. About 60,000 Sikh men, women and children were moving to safety in Malwa.

Abdali decided to make a lightning march. He crossed two rivers and covered a distance of more than 150 kilometers in just two days. The cavalry took the slow-moving Sikhs by surprise when they were near the village of Kup, about forty kilometers south of Ludhiana. The Sikhs were with their families and hence, were in a very vulnerable position. Some 30 thousand Sikhs were slaughtered by the well-equipped cavalry who had come with this very objective.

This massacre was the heaviest single blow that the Sikhs have had to withstand in their history. It is called *Wada Ghalughara,* or the Great Holocaust. Abdali also blew up the Harimandar Sahib and filled the Sarovar with refuse and dead cows to destroy the holy place, which he thought was the source of Sikh power.

The Sikhs recouped their strength again within months and fulfilled their statement, "The more we are cut, the more we grow." In May 1762, they took over Sirhind and in October 1762, on Diwali day, pushed Abdali out of Amritsar.

THE FEARLESS SIKHS

When Abdali invaded India for the seventh time in December 1764, there were only thirty Sikhs at Amritsar. Kazi Nur Mohd., a Muslim historian, writes that the Sikhs fought a fierce battle to the last man to defend their holy place. The Afghans then went berserk, they looted and devastated the areas as far as they could.

When Abdali started his journey home, it was the turn of the Sikhs to retrieve everything looted by him. While passing through Panjab, his guards trembled. They knew well that once the 'lions of Panjab' showed their faces to them, they would have to release the prisoners and forfeit all their possessions. Any resistance would mean the loss of their lives as well. Abdali witnessed all this but was helpless. The Sikhs would not face him in open battle, but with their sudden attacks would not leave him in peace either until he was out of the state. To instill confidence in his men, Abdali again and again uttered that he would turn the Sikhs into pulp.

After Abdali left for Afghanistan, the Sikhs were the lords of the stage again. The Khalsa occupied Lahore, but did no harm to the people or their property. This created a great respect for the Khalsa in the minds of the citizens. They accepted the Sikhs as their brave Panjabi brothers with high moral character. This image, built by the Khalsa after many sacrifices, opened the doors of the Panjab Raj to them. Afghans, though Muslims, were considered foreigners, looters and rapists even by the local Muslims. The outcome of this long struggle was the creation of the deep impression in the minds of the masses that the government was an aggressor and a tyrant. The people, therefore, challenged the authority of such a government and rejected its writ.

In April 1765, Sikhs gathered in Amritsar and decided to reconstruct Harimandar Sahib and protect it constantly from future desecration. *Amrit Sarovar* was cleaned. A lot of money was spend on rebuilding Harimandar Sahib and regular *Kirtan* was started there. The arrangements for *Guru Ka Langar* were expanded to keep pace with the increasing number of visitors who came to the holy city to pay homage. This is what the Sikhs had wished for more than half a century and for which un-parallel sacrifices had been made.

For the next two centuries the Harimandar Sahib remained under the control of the Sikhs. The structure, built in 1765, and plated in gold by Maharaja Ranjit Singh, stood inviolate until 1984, a symbol of human rights and the brotherhood of man throughout the world.

In 1984, the holy place was once again invaded and demolished. The Harimandar Sahib Complex was heavily damaged, this time not by any avowed enemy force but by the forces of the Republic of India, a nation created in 1947 from the sacrifices of several generations of freedom fighters, predominantly Sikhs. This invasion shocked Sikhs throughout the world because it was carried out by a government considered by them to be their own national government. In the tradition of all the other invasions, filth was thrown into the Sarovar, gold artifacts were looted, and more than six thousand men, women, and children were butchered. In addition, valuable rare books and manuscripts, including original writings of the Gurus, were deliberately destroyed. Once again, the Sikhs, a people who stood for truth, justice, and freedom of thought and who refused to compromise on these issues, had proved too much a threat to the ruling powers.

The Indian Government attempted to soothe the outraged feelings of the Sikhs worldwide and rebuilt the Akal Takht. However, the Sikhs demolished these repairs because an authority, which had committed such outrages against truth and justice, could not be allowed to leave its mark on the Akal Takht. In fact, work on a Sikh religious place can be carried out only by the Sikhs, working together collectively and not by governments or private people on individual initiative.

GOVERNORSHIP TO THE KHALSA

The lure of Indian wealth was very strong and it could not be resisted by the Afghans. Abdali crossed the Indus for the eighth time in November 1766 to attack India and take possession of Delhi. As soon as Abdali entered Panjab, the Sikhs vacated Lahore, as they had no army to pit against the invaders. They were ruling Lahore with just the goodwill of the people.

When Abdali reached Lahore, he found to his surprise that the local people had great respect and regard for the Sikhs. A deputation of the residents convinced him that offering governorship of Panjab to the Sikhs was the only means by which peace could be restored to the state. Abdali sent an invitation to Bhai Lehna Singh to rule Panjab on his behalf. Singh had moved to the forest after vacating the city and declined the offer. While returning the valuable gifts and the offer of governorship sent by Abdali to the Sikhs, Bhai Lehna Singh informed him, "We Sikhs live on jungle berries and do not need valuable fruit." The real reason for declining the offer was that the Khalsa were independent rulers of the state through their service to the people. They had no reason to be the subordinates of the Kabul regime.

The Khalsa again started collecting *Rakhi*, a kind of revenue, from the people as soon as Abdali was out of the Panjab. The authority of the governor was confined only to the limits of the city of Lahore. He had little control over the villages.

In 1769, during his ninth attempt to take over Panajb, Abdali was disappointed to find that it was truly the land of the Sikhs. He was not allowed even to cross the river Jhelum. Abdali, a terror for the emperors of Delhi, was a helpless sorrowful man before the Khalsa. He had to return to his country bitterly disappointed and give up forever any hope of annexing Panjab. This weighed very heavy on his heart and he died in 1772.

85

THE RULE OF THE KHALSA

Having defeated the Afghans in open battle, the Sikhs, under the leadership of Baba Baghel Singh, attacked Delhi and conquered it in 1783. Shah Alam was the ruler of Delhi. His Begam saved the reputation of her husband by becoming an honorary sister to the Sikhs. Accordingly, the Sikhs were honored by Shah Alam and given concessions, which could be considered signs of Shah Alam's generosity rather than those of his defeat. Baghel Singh was received with welcome in the Red Fort, and funds from the government revenues were allocated for building of gurdwaras at several Sikh historical places in Delhi, and for the regular maintenance of the Khalsa army. *It was during this time that Sis Ganj, Rakab Ganj, Bangla Sahib and other gurdwaras were built in Delhi. Muslims had orginally built mosques at the sites of Sis Ganj and Rakab Ganj.* These had to be dismantled to the general objections of the Muslim populace; still Shah Alam permitted the Sikhs to build their gurdwaras there, being connected with the martyrdom of the ninth Guru.

It is evident that the Sikhs had much power at that time. Had they all united and organized themselves under one command, they might have ruled all northern India and prevented the British from taking over Delhi. However, Baghel Singh left Delhi to return to the administration of his own region. In addition to the historical gurdwaras, there are some places in Delhi, which are connected with Baghel Singh. Tis Hazari, which means thirty thousand, is a well known place in Delhi where Baghel Singh camped with 30 thousand of his men. Pul Mithhai (the bridge of sweets) is a place where the General held sweets-making competitions.

Misls (divisions of the Khalsa) ruled Panjab until Maharaja Ranjit Singh united them many years later through a mixture of reason and force. Ranjit Singh entered Lahore on July 7, 1799 when he was 18 years old. Most of the credit goes to his mother-in-law, Rani Sada Kaur of the Kanhya Misl. He was declared Maharaja on April 12, 1801 by Sahib Singh Bedi. He enentually expanded his rule as far as the Sutlej in the east, Jammu and Kashmir including Ladakh in the north, and Multan province in the south. For the first time Panjabis managed to defeat Afghans and Pathans, leading to the Sikh occupation of Attock in July

1813. In 1819 they entered Peshawar in the west. Ranjit Singh established a secular administration. Many Muslims and Hindus held responsible and key posts. Ranjit Singh's generosity and broadmindedness are widely acknowledged by historians. There was no capital punishment during his rule in Panjab.

Since the Khalsa government was run personally by Ranjit Singh, it collapsed with his death. There was no person strong and competent enough to replace him in the management of his huge kingdom. The institution of the Khalsa Panth, the political arm of the Sikhs, could have administered the kingdom, had it not been rendered ineffective by Ranjit Singh's policy of taking decisions independently of the Guru Khalsa Panth. During the raj of Ranjit Singh, the Akal Takht and the Khalsa Panth had jurisdiction over religious affairs only.

Dhian Singh and Gulab Singh, two Dogras, held prominent positions in the government at Lahore. Through an understanding with the British rulers of Delhi, they fomented hostilities among members of Ranjit Singh's family. They were disloyal to the Sikhs and they virtually handed over Panjab to the British. As a reward, the British allowed them the raj of Jammu and Kashmir states. It was their descendant Hari Singh, Maharaja of Jammu and Kashmir, who opted to join India after the partition of the country in 1947.

CHAPTER VI

RENAISSANCE OF SIKH FAITH

A slow erosion of the Sikh character of the gurdwaras took place during the eighteenth century. The Khalsa had to leave their villages and move to the forests to seek safety from the police violence. The Sikh religious places were, therefore, cared for by the *Sahejdharis,* the non-turbaned devotees. After accepting the Sikh faith they, however, continued to follow Hindu rituals and thus unwittingly brought them to the gurdwaras. Later, it proved very difficult to screen out non-Sikh practices since they had been there for a long time and had shifted into all aspects of Sikh life. Baba Sahib Singh Bedi, who declared Ranjit Singh the Maharaja, wore *Janju* or sacred thread of Hinduism, a practice which Guru Nanak had firmly refused to follow.

With the British rule came Christian missionaries. Their enthusiasm awakened Sikh intellectuals for bringing Sikhs back to an awareness of the basic tenets of their religion. Therefore, during the last quarter of the nineteenth century, many Sikh organizations such as the Singh Sabhas and Khalsa Dewans were formed to safeguard Sikh religious and educational interests. These organizations bickered amongst themselves, but did much work to clarify Sikh beliefs. The Singh Sabhas in different regions of the state were interested in gurdwara reform. They formed a central body and endeavored to rid the gurdwaras of Hindu rituals, which contravened the teachings of the Gurus.

In 1905 Bhai Kahn Singh Nabha advised the British government representative in Amritsar to order the removal of Hindu idols from the *Parkarma* or causeway around the *Sarovar* of the Harimandar Sahib. However, the managers of the gurdwaras, who by now held these positions by right of heredity, resisted such attempts by the Singh Sabha movement. These hereditary managers, called Mahants, relied upon income provided by Hindus who followed those rituals. Gurdwara reform jeopardized this income. Sikh reformers were angered by the Mahants who often seemed more interested in their incomes than in the practice of Sikhism. In fact, many Mahants enjoyed lives of luxury and licentiousness far removed from the standards expected of religious leaders. Dislike of the Mahants united Sikhs on this common platform.

Meanwhile, the British began to be suspicious of the Singh Sabha movement. It was strengthening and unifying Sikhs at a time when the British right to rule in India was being challenged by many Indian thinkers. The British decided that the Sikhs, fast becoming a strong and cohesive group, must be denied control over the gurdwaras since these institutions were a source of money and of political and social influence. Therefore, the British government began to support the Mahants against the Singh Sabhas. In protest, the Sikhs converted their Gurdwara Reform Movement into a Gurdwara Freedom Movement. In other words, Sikhs decided to wrest gurdwara control from the Mahants entirely into their own hands.

Of course, the Gurdwara Freedom Movement was a direct challenge to the British, who in the early twentieth century represented the strongest political power in the world. They had just emerged victorious from World War I. The British government was conscious that an area as large and strategically placed as Panjab, if not completely under their control, could cause great problems for British supremacy. Thus the British were determined to squash any movement for more rights in Panjab.

VIOLENCE BY THE STATE

The first confrontation between the Sikhs and the British occured at Delhi. British government headquarters were moved from Calcutta to New Delhi in 1911. A wall of the Gurdwara Rakab Ganj was demolished in 1914 to allow the completion of the secretariat complex according to plan. The Sikhs protested strongly in large gatherings all over the state. The government promised that this wall would be rebuilt after the war. However, this promise was not fulfilled. Sikhs were angered especially because Sikh contributions to the British war in terms of soldiers and money had been very high, far out of proportion to their numbers in the population of India.

Sikhs announced that if the government failed to rebuild the wall, they would build it themselves. This threat of *Morcha* (moral struggle) forced the government to construct the wall at their own cost in 1921 at the original place. This was a great victory for the Sikhs.

The situation in Panjab, however, was handled tactlessly. In April 1919, the government took violent action against a group of people who were demonstrating peacefully against the Rowlatt Act. The Act contained drastic provisions for arrest or trial of Indians. Some of the demonstrators were killed. Several days later, on April 13, 1919, a large unarmed and peaceful crowd gathered in Jallianwala Bagh, Amritsar in a demonstration or *Satyagrah* against these killings. Around four hundred people were killed and one thousand injured when the police indiscriminately fired on them without warning. Of course, violent feelings against the government became much more widespread as a result of the Jallianwala Bagh incident. In fact, Jallianwala Bagh became a symbol for the Sikhs, rather for all people, of the need for India to gain control over its own affairs.

In this charged atmoshpere the Sikhs continued their agitation to regain control of their gurdwaras. They suffered great losses in struggle after struggle during this period.

On October 12, 1920 the priests in charge of the Harimandar Sahib refused the offerings of the Sikhs who were recent converts from the so-called untouchable caste. The refusal was in direct contrast to Sikh philosophy, and enraged the Sikh population. Some students under the guidance of the professors at the Khalsa College, Amritsar, travelled in fury to the Harimandar Sahib and caused the priests to flee in panic. The Sikhs gathered at Akal Takht on November 15, 1920, and established a temporary committee of 175 members to manage the gurdwaras. This was the first big success of the Sikhs in Panjab. Sikhs started occupying gurdwaras and organizing local Singh Sabhas to manage them. Some gurdwaras were handed over to them through goodwill. Other gurdwaras, where the Mahants did not cooperate, were taken by social pressure and force. In such cases, many Sikhs had to fight and lay down their lives. On December 14, 1920, the Akali Dal, the political arm of the Sikhs, was organized.

At Nankana Sahib, the visitors to the gurdwara were often insulted and women were even sexually assaulted. This gurdwara had a large estate attached to it. The Mahant had many vices and bad habits. However, he felt free to ignore Sikh sentiments because of the open support he enjoyed from the government. On February 20, 1921 about 150 unarmed Sikhs went to the gurdwara early in the morning. The Mahant's supporters who had been kept in the gurdwara to teach a lesson to the Singh Sabhias, as the reformer Sikhs were called during those days, closed the main gate. They shot, knifed and even burnt alive this group of Sikh pilgrims. When the Sikh population heard of this massacre, thousands walked long distances to Nankana Sahib. They were forced to go by foot because train travel was prohibited to them. The Sikhs were determined to take charge, at any cost, of the gurdwara and of the dead bodies of the Sikhs who had been massacred the day before.

After the massacre, the army had been ordered by the British government to occupy the gurdwara and had no intention of relinquishing their hold to the Sikhs. However, the good senses prevailsed. The Mahant and his men were taken into custody by the police. Sikhs took charge of the gurdwara and of the bodies of the massacred Sikhs, which were partly burnt and scattered everywhere.

The government continued to throw obstacles in the path of the Sikhs wanting to manage their religious affairs. On November 22, 1921, the government confiscated the keys of the Tosha Khana or fortified room for storage of valuables and relics of the Harimandar Sahib in Amritsar. The Sikhs protested and hundreds of them, including Baba Kharak Singh, the leader of the movement, were sent to jail.

The government finally agreed to hand back the keys if a representative of the Sikhs was sent to the office of the Deputy Commissioner in Amritsar. The Sikhs demanded that, since the keys had been taken by the government, they should be returned in the same way, the British representative bringing the keys to the Harimandar Sahib. At last on January 17, 1923, in spite of the claim that it had full authority over the gurdwaras, a representative of the empire returned the keys in person to the Akal Takht. It was another great victory for the Sikhs, the fruit of their sacrifices.

The government tried once again to show its power, but was caught up in an even more serious conflict with the Sikhs. By then, many gurdwaras had been brought under the control of the Akalis, the reformer Sikhs. Guru Ka Bagh, twenty kilometers from Amritsar, was still controlled by a Mahant. The government felt that he could be used to defeat the Akalis. The government invited a confrontation with the Sikhs by encouraging the Mahant

91

to prohibit the Sikhs from cutting wood in the Guru Ka Bagh. The place was actually in the possession of the Sikhs but technically under the control of the Mahant.

Wood from Guru Ka Bagh had been used for cooking *Langar* in the gurdwara at Amritsar for more than three centuries, ever since the time of the Gurus. Of course, the Akalis asserted their right to cut the wood for the *Langar.* The government sent a heavy police force to drive back the Akalis and protect the Mahant. Akalis with hands folded and heads lowered suffered cruel and merciless beatings by the police and trampling by police horses. (The deputy superintendent police, known as B.T. who committed the horrors was shot dead in Sunam by Kartar Singh.) Witnesses to this Morcha of August 12 to November 17, 1922 were horrified by the beatings and awed by the conduct of the Sikhs.

After 5600 Sikhs had been imprisoned and thousands incapacitated with broken limbs, the government finally admitted that the Sikhs had full rights over the Bagh.

THE CLIMAX

During the course of the Guru Ka Bagh struggle, Sikhs were involved in another confrontation elsewhere. On October 30, 1922, an incident occurred which shook the world. Sikh prisoners captured from Guru Ka Bagh were being transferred by train from Amritsar. The train carrying them was to pass through the Sikh holy place, Panja Sahib. The Sikhs approached the manager of the railway station to stop the train so that the hungry Sikh prisoners could be fed. When the stationmaster, under government orders, refused their request, the Sikh *Sangat* sat on the railway line to force the train to stop. The train came at full speed and ran over Bhai Karam Singh and Bhai Partap Singh, and then came to a halt. The Sikhs achieved their goal, of course, after making a great sacrifice.

Another struggle, which began before the Guru Ka Bagh Morcha ended, was at gurdwara Gang Sar, Jaito, which was then in Nabha State. The Sikhs wanted to recite Akhand Path there to pray for the restoration of the Maharaja of Nabha who had been deposed for showing sympathy for the Sikh cause. The struggle started on a low key in September 1923, but was heightened when the government detained all the Sikhs in the gurdwara reciting Gurbani. The peaceful struggle attracted the attention of the national leaders. Jawahar Lal Nehru went to Nabha. He also was arrested and imprisoned. Nehru wrote :

> *I am happy to be charged for joining a cause owned by the Akalis. I was astonished to observe the bravery and sacrifices of the Sikhs in Guru Ka Bagh. I was waiting for a chance to appreciate them. I pray with my heart that I may live up to the high heritage of the Akalis—Sat Sri Akal.*

The Gurdwara Committee conducting the Morcha at Gurdwara Gang Sar was declared unlawful on October 12, 1923 and its members were arrested. Some members evaded arrest and continued to guide the Morcha program. However when demanded by the government, they turned themselves over to the authorities in January 1924, as an act of sacrifice. Even without the leaders, the Sikhs continued their struggle for religious freedom. By January 1924 the property of ninety Sikhs had been confiscated as punishment for support of the Morcha. More than 12,000 people were warned to "behave", and threatened with severe punishment if they sympathized with the Sikhs.

This Morcha took a serious turn on February 21, 1924, when a *Jatha* of five hundred Sikhs, moving peacefully towards the gurdwara and reciting Gurbani, were moved down by machine gun fire. About 150 Sikhs were killed and many of the dead were burnt to conceal the fact of their death. This act of terror committed by the state government was denounced in the assembly of the central government in Delhi as a shameful act. Undaunted by the massacre, another *Jatha* of five hundred Sikhs approached the gurdwara. This group instead of being attacked by bullets was arrested and imprisoned. Other groups continued to work for the Morcha to put pressure on the central government to change its policy of confrontation.

THE VICTORY

(I) THE GURDWARA ACT

After many years of struggle, invoking physical and financial sacrifices on the part of thousands of Sikhs, the Sikhs became victorious. The British government agreed that Sikhs should have control over their own religious places. **According to the statement made in the Panjab Legislative Council 30,000 Sikhs were arrested, 2000 wounded and 1100 killed during this** struggle. **A fine of one and a half million rupees was inflicted and pensions of Sikhs retired from the army or civil services were forfeited.** The proportion of Sikhs in the army was reduced from 20% to 13% in 1930.

The Sikh Gurdwara Act was approved on July 18, 1925. The Shiromani Gurdwara Parbandhak Committee, the first elected body of the Sikhs, was legally recognized in November 1926. It was given sovereign rights over the management and control of the gurdwaras.

(II) SIKH SACRIFICES HONORED

Father Andrews, a Christian priest, cried when he saw the cruelties inflicted on the unarmed hymn-singing Sikhs. He said, **"I see hundreds of Christs being crucified everyday."** Moti Lal Nehru, the father of Jawahar Lal Nehru, the first Prime Minister of India said, **"I salute the Sikhs who are fighting for freedom."** Madan Mohan Malvya said, **"The freedom movement has been born at Guru Ka Bagh. It will lead to freedom for the whole of India."** He added, **"Each family in India should make one son adopt the Sikh faith."**

When this mighty empire bowed down to the Sikhs, Dr. Saffudin Kitchlew commenced, **"Our Sikh brothers have taught us the way to achieve freedom. No power can stop us now, from becoming a free nation."** Mohandas Karamchand Gandhi telegraphed the Sikhs, **"Congratulations. The first battle of Indian freedom has been won."**

AFTER THE VICTORY

Unfortunately, a difference of opinion arose in the Sikh community over the conditions for the release of the Sikhs and provisions of the Gurdwara Act. Some Sikhs led by Teja Singh Samundari foresaw the shortcomings of the Act and the conditions laid down by the government for their release from jail. They, therefore, refused to accept it, even though this meant their continued imprisonment. Samundari died in jail on July 17, 1926. Those Sikhs who approved the Act were released as part of the agreement with the government.

When the first election to the Shiromani Gurdwara Parbandhak Committee was held, the problems Sardar Samundari envisaged became reality. Those who had supported each other through the years of struggle now fought tooth and nail among themselves for berths in the newly established Sikh body, and the Khalsa Panth was split wide open. Eventually Master Tara Singh, the leader of the Sikhs, published an article in his monthly magazine Sant-Sipahi. It was concerning his dissatisfaction with the elected committee system and the prevailing corruption among the committee employees. The building constructed to accommodate the Committee's head office was named Teja Singh Samundari Hall in memory of the man who died in jail rather than accepting conditional release as desired by the government.

The Committee did an excellent job in many ways. They appointed a sub-committee on religious affairs. They screened the prevailing practices in the gurdwaras and printed a booklet, *Sikh Reht Maryada*. It describes the standard practices for uniform adoption by Sikhs all over the world. In memory of the Sikh martyrs, a Shaheed Sikh Missionary College was established at Amritsar to train Sikh scholars and teachers. A Khalsa College in Bombay and the Guru Nanak Engineering College, Ludhiana, were also established by the Committee. Guru Ram Das School and Guru Ram Das Hospital at Amritsar are other important achievements of the Committee. Of course, managing the gurdwaras and preaching Sikh heritage are the routine responsibilities of the Committee.

Today (1988), the people feel that Sikh character had been at its highest when Sikhs struggled against injustice. Gradually, once they had gained control of their religious centers, their bright image began to tarnish. Some leaders allowed selfish motives to overcome their principles. They bartered their high character for government positions. Some persons sought membership in the Committee, not as an occasion to serve the Panth, but as a spring board to election to the Panjab assembly. The prestige of the Akal Takht was lowered because the Jathedar or the Chief Executive was more an employee of the Committee than a person acting in the interest of the Khalsa.

Hunger for power replaced the zeal for service, which prevailed during the agitation. Sincere Sikhs watched helplessly as some of their associates against the wishes of the Panth joined the ruling Congress party. They used their government influence to interfere in gurdwara management against the interest of the Sikhs and Sikhism.

Some members of the Gurdwara Management Committee.

adopted practices decried in its bulletin, the *Sikh Reht Maryada*. Sikhs began to feel that Committee management did not come up to their expectations. Committee members who should be the servants of the Panth considered themselves to be the masters.

The horror of June 1984, when the Indian army invaded the sacred Harimandar Sahib, is expected to bring forward the Khalsa members who are interested in the honor of the Panth and not in their self-aggrandizement. They will not use the Panth for their own glory but will offer their lives for the glory of the Panth as Sikhs have done in the past.

> *(Unfortunately, before the celebrations of the third centennial in 1999 the leadership of the Panth was split. The overbearing presence of the government and Hindutva forces was quite obvious during the celebrations. The politically ambitious Sikhs took control of the religious bodies and misused them for their selfish interests. It further tarnished the glory of the Panth. Let us pray that visionary and sincere Sikhs would come forward to retrieve the pristine glory of the Panth.)*

CHAPTER VII

SIKHISM REACHES THE WEST

Sikhs migrated in small numbers to the West in the last years of the nineteenth century and the early twentieth century. Mass scale immigration to Great Britain occurred after World War II, when men were needed to run the industries there. Being hard-working people, they made a good living for themselves and invited their relatives to settle there. Many of them gave up their identity, uncut hair and turban, to assimilate into the local people. Now, Sikhs are playing a significant role there in social,. political, and economic fields. The second generation of the immigrant Sikhs is well set in various professional fields. They have proved themselves to be good doctors, engineers, industrialists and businessmen. A large number of them are employed in blue-collar jobs.

Early visitors to North America settled mostly on the Pacific coast in California and British Columbia. They established gurdwaras in Stockton, Vancouver, and other cities. When in 1912 a formal flag hoisting ceremony was to be performed at Stockton, European residents gathered there to oppose the raising of the Sikh flag on American land. A young Sikh leader, Professor Teja Singh, (later, Sant Teja Singh of Mustuana) a graduate of Harvard University and president of the Pacific Coast Society of Sikhs, addressed the gathering. He used public address system to reach the protesters outside the gurdwara. He explained to them that Sikhism is a universal message and aims at welfare of whole humanity. The Sikh flag is a symbol of the religion rather than a rival to the American national flag. The Americans were pacified and they joined the Sikh *sangat* for the inaugural function. The Sikhs thus established their first gurdwara with the goodwill of the local population.

After World War II, there was a big increase in the flow of Indian intellectuals to America in search of higher education. Because of it they could cliam influential positions in India. Many of these intellectuals, finding better opportunities in

America and Canáda, settled there and invited their friends and relatives to join them.

At present it is estimated that there are more than one million Sikhs in the United States, Canada, Britain and other European countries. The whole world is acquainted with the Sikhs because of their unique appearance. Sikhs are no more strangers in any major city of the world. Their performance has earned them a good reputation as respectable citizens. The world knows them as very brave soldiers, good sportsmen, competent professionals, good workers and affectionate friends.

Every person in a new social, cultural or geographical environment faces many problems. Sikhs have had to face such problems more so because of their distinct appearance. However, Sikhs have adapted themselves to their new environment wherever they have settled. They have contributed their best in the fields of arts and science. They have adopted new places as their homes and have mixed well with society. This has helped them to earn a respectable place among the local people.

INFLUENCE OF THE WESTERN CULTURE

Sikhs migrating to the West retained their love for the Sikh faith. However, an appreciable number of them could not retain the Sikh uniform for a longer time. Every person who formally accepts Sikhism by taking *Amrit* has to retain the five K uniform, read the hymns regularly and adopt the life prescribed for a Sikh. Many of them were not even able to continue to follow the routine practices of Sikhism. The major problem of the immigrant Sikhs was keeping their hair uncut and retaining their turban. People, seeing a Sikh for the first time, could not help staring at him, and making him feel self-conscious of his unique appearance. Many Sikhs feel uncomfortable attracting this much attention.

(ii) Earliest Sikh immigrants reached North America by the turn of the century. They were ex-army men who had served the British as proud Sikh soldiers overseas, while maintaining their uncut hair and turbans. These pioneers were committed to their faith and retained their symbols when they settled along the Pacific coast from Vancouver to Los Angeles. Sawmill owners and other employers favored these men because of their physical fitness, sincerity and attitude for hard work. They earned money and built their gurdwaras in British Columbia and California. All office bearers were *Amritdhari*. They also took an active part in organizing freedom movement against British imperialism and founded the Ghadar party.

Sikh symbols were no hindrance for getting a job by the immigrants during those days. The white workers did protest against the Sikhs for providing cheap labor and thus reducing their chances of employment. Discarding symbols started in 1915 when many dedicated Sikhs left Canada to join the freedom movement in India. Some of those left behind removed their turbans to avoid their visibility while crossing the USA border to save themselves from being caught and deported.

In 1924, about 300 illegal Sikh immigrants removed their turbans to conceal their identity before entering into Canada. Their arrival reduced the turbaned Sikhs to a minority. It decreased the guilty feeling connected with the removal of turbans. **However, the constitution of the Khalsa Diwan Society continued to retain the Amritdhari clause. Because of the majority of Sikhs without turbans, this clause was removed in 1952 and those who wanted to retain this clause founded Akali Singh Gurdwara in Vancouver.**

In the mid 1970's, a young man having got a M.A. degree from Panjab, came to Vancouver. He was advised to cut his hair because it was a requirement for getting a job. He was not even given a ride for finding his job unless he cuts his hair. Finally, he was able to convince someone to take him to a lumber mill for seeking employment. The youth completed the application form and handed it over to the foreman. After reading his application, he immediately offered him the job. Having gotten the appointment papers in his hand, the youth addressed the foreman, "May I ask you a question ?" Hearing "yes" from the foreman, he continued, "Will there be any objection to retaining my turban and hair ?" The foreman replied, **"We do not object to anyone wearing a turban. It is one's own choice."** When he returned home his friends felt embarrassed for misguiding him that cutting hair was essential for getting a job. They confessed, **"Your uncut hair and turban are constant reminder to us for our failure to keep them. Now we give you an important and correct advice. Some of your friends will press you for drinking alcohol. Do not touch it, even if they**

force you to take a little sip. You will be happy."

(ii) In search of jobs, Sikhs spread out all over North America. Being so thinly spread, most of the Sikhs did not have a gurdwara within their easy access. Furthermore, the fast pace and pressure of life in the West meant that their lives were taken up with their work and social obligations. Some became over-involved with the pleasures that their new lives had to offer. For various reasons, then, many Sikhs gave up their five K symbols and the regular reading of Gurbani.

In the West, drinking alcohol is not regarded as a sin; rather it is a central part of many social gatherings. Sikhs, to gain acceptance in the community, drank liquor with their friends, even though Sikhs are expected to avoid alcohol and narcotics.

As the number of immigrating Sikhs increased, gurdwaras were gradually built in the major cities and organized Sikh life became available to more and more Sikhs. In every organization, at one time or another, the question arose whether the so-called "Shaved Sikhs" should enjoy the same position in the gurdwaras as Sikhs who maintain the five Ks. For example, whether or not anyone but a fully bearded and turbaned Sikh should hold office in a gurdwara formed a controversial issue within many organizations. As a result, many Sikh *Sangats* and organizations developed serious rifts, which were deepened by personal and political differences.

PLEA FOR CUTTING HAIR

(i) Many Sikhs, who have cut their hair, believe that it was only for the days of fighting against the Mughals that the Guru wished Sikhs to identify themselves with uncut hair. It is not obligatory for every Sikh to keep hair, particularly in the days of peace. They say that, in any case, they are simply Sikhs who follow the first nine Gurus, who at no time established a requirement of uncut hair. Furthermore, they point out that Kesh is only one of the five symbols that the Sikhs must maintain and accordingly less significant than Sikhs with uncut hair claim it is. Sikhs who attempt to justify the cutting of their hair also argue that in modern times, it is enough to follow the principles of the Sikh faith and to live an honest life. According to them, they are following in the tradition of the *Sehajdhari,* or "slow adopting" Sikhs. These Sikhs managed the gurdwaras during the

18th century while the Khalsa Sikhs, with uncut hair, lived in the forest and deserts for safety. Only Khalsa Sikhs, the members of the Sikh 'army' they claim, need adopt the Sikh symbols.

Sikhs, who argue in this fashion, are ignoring several important facts about Sikhism. The *Amrit* ceremony held by the last Guru in 1699 made it obligatory for every Sikh to maintain the five Sikh symbols, including un-cut hair. A Sikh has no option in the matter of keeping his/her hair un-cut. A Christian wears his religious symbol, a cross, if this custom gives him personal satisfaction, but a Sikh keeps the five Sikh symbols because the Guru himself, emphatically and unambiguously, prescribed this practice for the Sikhs. The teachings of the first nine gurus were not different from those of the tenth Guru. The people who followed the earlier Gurus were given a stronger definition by Guru Gobind Singh through the institution of the five Ks. Their acceptance of these symbols was a pledge to live according to Sikh principles.

(ii) Some people of Sikh background who cut their hair do not try to develop a philosophical justification for this action. *They accept that keeping the five Ks is essential for a Sikh, but they claim realities of the Western environment force them to cut their hair against their wishes.* However, this argument does not stand close examination. A young Sikh, who had wanted distinction in tennis, cut his hair saying that he needed to do so to fit into North American society. His excuse, surely, is rather hollow, since while wearing a turban he had already become a State level champion. Cutting his hair wasn't as much a result of social pressure as lack of attachment to the five Ks. Further, there was no reason to blame his turban indiscriminately for all the inevitable problems which arose in his day to day social interactions.

High scholastic, athletic, or professional achievement, of course, is not the most important goal for Sikhs. A Sikh who enjoys a prestigious positions in society because of such achievements considers it secondary to his wish to uphold truth and justice in his daily life. Still it is encouraging to the average person to learn that a life of dedication to Sikhism does not involve renunciation of the world. On the contrary, it demands full participation in society.

There are many Sikhs who have retained their five Ks and still contributed largely to Western society. At any rate, if the Western environment was solely responsible for the Sikhs removing their turbans, how can it be explained that the local Americans who become Sikhs wear turbans proudly and raise their children to do so.

Furthermore, the Western environment cannot be the main reason that Sikhs cut their hair, since this tendency of the Sikhs is not confined to the West. A large number of young Sikhs in Panjab, cut their hair or at least trim their beards. The author, during his visit to the villages in Panjab found in some cases more than half the male children with their hair cut. The male children whose hair was un-cut, were likely to conform to the practice of their un-turbaned friends as they grew up. (Of course, the government invasion of the Harimandar Sahib in 1984 has caused a renewal of faith among Sikhs and many have re-adopted the five K symbols.)

Apathy toward the five Ks is not, then, a function of the Western environment only. The real reason is that some possess a stronger pull toward conformity with the rest of the population than their wish to practice Sikh principles.

In the eighteenth century, Sikhs faced death when they kept their hair uncut; Sikhs in the West are not facing as great a risk as that. Those Sikhs who lived in the forests believed that the Sikh symbols were a unique gift to humanity. To them, it was a great privilege to keep the five Ks. The rational and practical philosophy of Sikhism is highly regarded by several modern scholars who recognize that Sikhism is a religion applicable to all humanity. Sikhs should be proud of their religion and stimulated by the opportunity to participate in such a noble tradition.

It is probable that many young people from Sikh background would adopt the five Ks if they were more aware of the spiritual and moral benefits which derive from the following of the Sikh faith. Sometimes a young person of Sikh background whose family has relinquished the five Ks receives his only exposure to Sikh principles from traditional scholars. They are out of touch with the Western way of life and they do not see the necessity of showing how Sikh principles are relevant to modern times. Often, when young people question the value of five Ks, they are met with rage, rather than with an attempt to explain the five Ks in terms which are meaningful to them. Instead of developing a dialogue with young people, some Sikh scholars dismiss those who have questioning minds as "lost people",

In fact, Sikhs, both young and old, should be encouraged to discuss issues. No person should be denigrated because of his opinions. However, whether or not a Sikh should have uncut hair is not a matter of opinion. Guru Gobind stated most emphatically that to be a Sikh, a person must maintain the five Ks as his/her identity. **One has a choice of whether to be or not to be a Sikh, but, if the choice is to be a Sikh, the decision automatically includes uncut hair.**

CASE HISTORIES

(i) It might be surprising that the school-going Sikh youth, who keep their hair uncut, face less discrimination than might be expected. Often, an explanation to the school principal that Sikhs are required for religious reasons to keep their hair uncut is all that may be needed to ease a child's progress through school. Turbaned Sikhs have taken top honors in their schoolwork, and won distinction in school sports. Many young people have found that wearing a turban makes them morally strong, courageous, and hard working, since they are always conscious of living up to the requirements of Sikhism.

A young elementary school boy earned a place of honor for himself and his faith by excelling at soccer. He won distinctions and prizes for his school and became known to many people in the neighbourhood. The parents were asked by many persons why their son had long hair while the father himself had cut hair. The father explained so many times that his son's uncut hair was a symbol of his religion, but that he himself had cut his hair for reasons of social pressure, that he finally decided to leave his own hair un-cut. He found that the problem, he thought he had to face with turban on his head, did not exist at all. It was due to the lack of self-confidence that he had cut his hair.

Another young boy withstood the ridicule of his schoolmates and kept his turban through four school changes. He won many prizes at the anuual school function and impressed others by his strength of mind and dedication to Sikhism. Because of this, four other Sikh boys of his school were motivated to keep their hair uncut. The Sikh children observed that having a unique appearance was a distinction rather than an embarrassment. **Feeling guilty for not conforming to others is a self-inflicted punishment. A turban is a matter of pride for the wearer. It is a symbol of his faith in universal brotherhood and equality of humanity.**

Some communities, in fact, are happy to receive turbaned Sikhs into their midst. They often feature the families in local newspapers, and display a lively interest in understanding the Sikh religion. However, when a Sikh looks for employment, he may run into some obstacles.

In California, a mother was tired of explaining to her son day after day why she wanted him to keep his hair. Finally, when he asked her, as he did frequently, for permission to cut his hair, she told him to bring the scissors, and that she herself would cut his hair. The son was, of course, astonished that she hadn't told him, as usual, that a Sikh would rather lose his head than cut his hair. Then his mother, reminded him that, although it would be easy to cut his hair, it would be impossible to change the color of his skin. Consequently, the white Americans, to whom he was apparently trying to conform, still would not accept him fully. She told him, "Since you can never be the same as they are, remain what you are, work hard, and become superior to them."

In this way, the boy was shown that his different appearance made him inferior only if he allowed it to. Therefore, he became determined to earn people's respect. He graduated from high school with prizes for both his sports achievements and his academic work. The white students, whom he wanted to resemble, showed great respect for him and his parents. The boy was convinced that his turban was no hindrance in being popular with his friends.

(ii) **Sometimes even 'Sikhs' who have cut their hair ridicule other Sikhs who insist on maintaining the five Ks.** This pressure from Sikh brothers is more often the reason for breaking the will of many Sikhs to retain their long hair. Self-esteem and firm determination of a Sikh strengthen his/her mind to face such internal attacks.

When a young Sikh from India landed in USA, he was

repeatedly told about the "serious problem" he would have to face with his beard and turban. Everyday, he was advised to go to the barber without any further delay. However, the young Sikh obtained admission for higher studies while retaining his turban and his faith. He was so much pressurized by his uncle that he had to move out of the house to remain a turbaned Sikh. His uncle later confessed that the very sight of the turban reminded him everyday of his guilt of discarding the sacred turban and his hair. He felt uneasy all day. Now, the uncle repents for having ignored his Sikh heritage because his children have adopted the western permissive life. They spend his wealth but don't listen to him. He feels he has lost them and has no hope of bringing them back to the track.

(iii) It cannot be denied that almost every Sikh has had the experience of being offered a job only on the condition that he remove his turban and cut his hair. Many find satisfying jobs in spite of those experiences. Some others have taken low-paying or low-prestige employment rather than give up the five Ks. Those who maintain their symbols in spite of difficulties often find that they become an inspiration to Sikhs who have cut their hair. **Many Sikhs recount how keeping their hair uncut caused them difficulties in the beginning. However, it eventually gave them an inner courage that made them morally strong, and incidentally, successful in a material sense as well.**

A Sikh doctor newly arrived in the United States was offered high paying employment if he cut his hair. He decided to decline the offer, because acceptance would mean exchanging his five Ks for filthy lucre. He took work, which paid a minimum wage and continued to live according to the Sikh *Reht* and superior values of life. One of his sons was badly harassed by children at school, but he handled the physical assaults courageously, until the principal intervened. Eventually, the son attained the highest academic standing in his school and the father was soon offered a professional job after recognizing his qualifications. Still they felt that their long struggle to maintain the five Ks had been justified, even if conditions had not improved for them.

In 1959, a Sikh with a Ph.D. degree from New York was unsuccessful in his search for a suitable job. The president of the university recommended him to many institutions for a suitbale job. However, he received negative responses because of the Sikh's beard and turban. Finally, the president advised him to cut his hair, and offered to pay for psychiatric treatment to help adjust to the change. The Sikh declined the offer politely. That was the last test for his commitment to the Sikh faith. The next day, he received a letter offering him a job with the United Nations. Today (1985) he is a distinguished professor in a university, still fully bearded and turbaned.

A clinical psychologist was offered work in a New York hospital on the condition that he cut his hair and beard. He refused and worked at a gas station for some months. In time, he found work, which was fitted to his qualifications, and now he is an eminent psychologist often invited to give seminars in Russia and Europe.

In 1984 a Sikh, who graduated with high marks from a medical school in India, was unable to find a hospital residency in USA. Finally, he was given a place in one of the very hospitals, which had recommended he remove his turban if he wanted to be accepted. In other words, his high standing overcame any reservation of the hospital staff concerning his unusual appearance.

All these examples show that a Sikh who wishes to keep his turban in the West can do so. A Sikh who cuts his hair does that by choice, and not because of the pressures of the environment.

(iv) Sometimes Sikhs give up their hair in the belief that Western society will accept them more easily, forgetting that the prejudice they face is not solely because of their turbans, but also as a result of the white dominated society disliking darker skin. **This, being a racial prejudice, exists whether a Sikh wears a turban or not.**

A third-generation Sikh endorsed the above statement after a long experience of living in Canada. He feels that the children of the immigrant Sikhs, for their peace and self-esteem, should live as Sikhs rather than imitate the European Canadians. His grand father came to Canada in 1906. Born in 1953, he is a fair colored European-looking man working as a chartered accountant and is well respected in his field. When the European Candidates come to know that he is an East Indian, their attitude towards him immediately changes. This happened to him so often in every day life that he decided to raise his son, the fourth-generation

Canadian, as a visible Sikh, with turban and uncut hair. He wants to give his son the pride of his faith and its great heritage, which one can enjoy only if he respects the Sikh symbols, the articles of the faith.

Refusing to give up the turban, and facing detractors proudly, has a profound effect on a Sikh's psychological make-up. He becomes confident and firm in his resolve to accomplish whatever he sets out to do. A Sikh, who kept his turban in America on the advice of a long-time south-Indian immigrant, is happy he chose as he did. His adviser had told him that if he simply acted as himself, he would be accepted by more people than if he tried to imitate others. Today, this Sikh agrees with that advice, and says, **"Everybody can swim with the tide, but only a courageous person can swim against it."** Such a life provides a sense of achievement of its own kind.

(v) In fact, Sikhs should remember that not every Westerner is prejudiced against them. Just after the Indian army attack on Harimandar Sahib in 1984, an American went into a doctor's office, having learned that the doctor's name was "Singh". When she saw that the doctor's hair was cut, she was surprised. She told him that she had expected to find a representative of the brave Sikh community but was disappointed. "Either grow your hair and beard", she said, "or remove your name *Singh* from your nameplate."

Thus, in the final analysis, Sikhs must maintain all five Sikh symbols, including uncut hair, in order to remain Sikhs. There is no philosophical justification for Sikhs cutting their hair, nor can it be said that the Western environment forces them to relinquish their turbans. If a Sikh cuts his hair, he can still be a good person and a supporter of the Sikh faith but he cannot be identified as a member of the Sikh Panth (Khalsa).

This Sikh requirement has been recognized by the governments of Canada and USA. The Sikh members of the R.C.M.P. Canada have already been allowed to wear their turbans while on duty.

In 1991, the author felt pleased and honored to talk to a young turbaned Sikh in Vancouver serving as a lieutenant in the Canadian forces. He passed all the stringent tests and went through the rigorous army training without any problem while retaining the articles of the faith.

We Sikhs should keep in mind that racial and ethnic prejudice exists all over the world even among the people of the same faith. The ruling white Christians in South Africa did not allow for a very long time equal civil rights to the local African Christians. In India, the so-called low caste often demonstrate for their equal social status and thousands have been killed during violent inter-caste fights. Residents of one province have strong prejudice against the language and people of the other province. Political demostrations were held in Tamil Nadu against forcing the use of Hindi in the state by the Indian government.

The unbiased analysis shows that prejudice is a world-wide phenomenon, it is not just against Sikhs alone because of their long hair and turban. It will not, therefore, go away even if a Sikh removes his turban. Hence, it is good for a Sikh to retain his turban, his identity and the article of his faith.

CHAPTER VIII
THE SIKH FAITH, A REVOLUTION

The study of the previous chapters reveals that Guru Nanak created a revolution in the field of religion. He revealed a totally 'new' God Who loves people of all faiths. The Guru also gave a new mission of life, that is, to accept all people as brothers and sisters irrespective of the name they adopt to love God. The philosophy and the code of conduct preached by the Gurus are summarized in this chapter.

(A) ALL HUMANITY IS ONE

The first message of Guru Nanak, "There is no Hindu, no Musalman; we are all equal humans and are **all loved by God**", shook the people and the religious leaders of different faiths. In the year 1499, it was a revolutionary thought in the field of faith. Nanak argued, "We cannot have two Gods, one who loves only the Hindus and the other who loves only the Muslims. God did not create Hindus or Muslims, He created humans. Of course, they are of different colors and of different forms in the same way as He created different kinds of flowers, all giving their own nice sweet smell and adding beauty to nature. God, being the sole Father, the Creator of the universe, equally loves all humans, whatever their language, their culture, and whatever the Name (Allah, Ram, Gobind, Guru, God) they adopt to address Him."

The belief of any religious group that they alone are entitled to go to Heaven and the followers of other faiths will go to Hell, was rejected by Guru Nanak.

One can imagine how such thoughts touched the traditional people. The Brahmans had preached for many centuries that among the Hindus they were the superior most human beings. The fighters, called Kshatryas, were placed next to them and the third position was given to the business community. People serving the three higher castes were considered Sudras, the low caste, hence were believed unfit for Heaven. According to the Brahmans, all lower castes were destined for Hell. Similarly, the Muslims considered *Bahisht* (Heaven) to be reserved for them alone. All non-Muslims were *Kafirs* and were destined for *Dozakh* (Hell).

However, the Guru denied that beyond this earth, somewhere else in the universe, there existed any particular places known as either Heaven or Hell to which our souls were headed. The reason most of us believe in religion is that after death we want to get admission to Heaven and are frightened of being thrown into Hell. The Guru said the goal of human life is not qualifying for admission into a non-existent Heaven or being scared of a mythological Hell. A person is in Hell when he ignores the presence of God within him and suffers from ego, hate, lust or anger. He enjoys the bliss of Heaven when he sings the virtues of God and loves His children, the human beings. (Chapter III).

Guru Nanak thus broke the barriers of faiths that had split people into mutually-hating sects and creeds. He preached that all people are equal human beings and none of them can be considered superior or inferior because of the variation in their color, race, culture or language. According to Guru Nanak, a holy person is he who accepts all people as his classmates; that is, he considers himself an equal member (neither inferior nor superior) of the big class called human beings.

ਆਈ ਪੰਥੀ ਸਗਲ ਜਮਾਤੀ ਮਨਿ ਜੀਤੈ ਜਗੁ ਜੀਤੁ ॥

(Guru Granth, p. 6)

The Guru decried the old Brahmanical rituals believed to help a man to reach Heaven. He said that adopting the creed of fake purity (something gets polluted if seen or touched by a low caste person), abandoning the family life for meditation, and reading scriptures to grasp the knowledge and intelligence therein, are of little use for realizing God. The path for realization of the goal of life is obedience to the Will of the Lord. In the first hymn of the Jap Ji, the Guru says it in these words;

ਸੋਚੈ ਸੋਚਿ ਨ ਹੋਵਈ ਜੇ ਸੋਚੀ ਲਖ ਵਾਰ ॥
ਚੁਪੈ ਚੁਪ ਨ ਹੋਵਈ ਜੇ ਲਾਇ ਰਹਾ ਲਿਵ ਤਾਰ ॥....
ਸਹਸ ਸਿਆਣਪਾ ਲਖ ਹੋਹਿ ਤਾ ਇਕ ਨ ਚਲੈ ਨਾਲਿ ॥
ਕਿਵ ਸਚਿਆਰਾ ਹੋਈਐ ਕਿਵ ਕੂੜੈ ਤੁਟੈ ਪਾਲਿ ॥
ਹੁਕਮਿ ਰਜਾਈ ਚਲਣਾ ਨਾਨਕ ਲਿਖਿਆ ਨਾਲਿ ॥

(Guru Granth, p. 1)

Further, the concluding hymn of the Jap Ji states :

ਕਰਮੀ ਆਪੋ ਆਪਣੀ ਕੇ ਨੇੜੈ ਕੇ ਦੂਰਿ ॥

110

ਜਿਨੀ ਨਾਮੁ ਧਿਆਇਆ ਗਏ ਮਸਕਤਿ ਘਾਲਿ ॥

ਨਾਨਕ ਤੇ ਮੁਖ ਉਜਲੇ ਕੇਤੀ ਛੁਟੀ ਨਾਲਿ ॥ (Guru Granth, p. 8)

It means we will be judged by our deeds and not by our beliefs. Anyone (a Hindu, a Muslim or a person of any other faith, a low caste, a rich person, a poor person, a scholar, or an illiterate, man or woman) who loves God can realize Him.

In other words, God is nobody's private inheritance; nobody can claim a franchise on Him. Forcing and torturing the weak to change their faith and method of worship is anti-God. It is like threatening a person to force him to address his/her father as 'Dad' and not as 'Papa'. Such actions are disapproved of by God.

A person, whatever his caste, faith, or social status, who said that God lives in all human beings, was accepted by the Guru to be a holy human. A close friend of Guru Nanak of his childhood age was Mardana, a Muslim, born in a so-called low caste. He was addressed as Bhai (brother) by Guru Nanak. The hymns of more than two dozen devotees of God (*Bhagats*) from different religions and speaking different languages were included in the holy scripture, Sri Guru Granth Sahib, to guide the life of the seekers of Truth. (See Chapter III). As observed in the introductory paragraphs, the hymns of this holy scripture are meant for all people. However, sometimes it is mistakenly considered to be a scripture for Sikhs alone. We know it well that chemistry, biology, and other sciences are meant not just for a country or a community but for anyone who wants to benefit from them. To learn and to benefit from the sciences, one is not obliged to be a follower of the scientists. One is not required even to identify himself as a formal scientist to take advantage of the knowledge provided by any of the sciences. Similarly, one is not required to believe in the Gurus or the *Bhagats* who wrote these hymns included in Sri Guru Granth Sahib, nor is one required to be a formal Sikh to take advantage of the path to God explained there. A rose is a rose called by any other name. God is our Father, our Lord; we all are His children, hence equal; of course, because of His Will, we have different cultures. Thus, there is only one faith for all the people; one may give it any name one likes. Rightly, this revelation has been called a revolutionary thought for the modern man to adopt and bring peace on this earth.

(B) GOD, THE FATHER OF ALL PEOPLE

So far, the preachers emphasized on conversion to "save" people of other faiths. They believed that their's was the only true faith and others were pagan faiths. However, Gurbani proclaimed that God is the Father of all humanity and not just for any one particular community alone. *God is nobody's private inheritance. No one can claim a monopoly on Him. He belongs to everyone.*

ਆਪਨ ਬਾਪੈ ਨਾਹੀ ਕਿਸੀ ਕੋ ਭਾਵਨ ਕੋ ਹਰਿ ਰਾਜਾ ॥

(Guru Granth, p. 658)

The Almighty Lord can be worshipped through innumerable languages and by innumerable names—Creator, Allah, Ram, Gobind, Guru, and God. All names are equal; no one name is superior or inferior. We may praise Him by any name and still gain acceptance by Him. *Those who love him achieve the goal of their human life.*

ਜਿਨੀ ਨਾਮੁ ਧਿਆਇਆ ਗਏ ਮਸਕਤਿ ਘਾਲਿ ॥

(Guru Granth, p. 8)

Guru Nanak revealed that only good deeds could save a soul on Judgement day. No prophet, Avtar, or a savior would be able to intercede. Without good deeds, all persons, whatever their faith, will have to repent.

ਪੁਛਨਿ ਫੋਲਿ ਕਿਤਾਬ ਨੋ ਹਿੰਦੂ ਵਡਾ ਕਿ ਮੁਸਲਮਾਨੋਈ?
ਬਾਬਾ ਆਖੇ ਹਾਜੀਆ ਸੁਭਿ ਅਮਲਾ ਬਾਝਹੁ ਦੋਨੋ ਰੋਈ ॥

(Bhai Gurdas, Var 1-33)

The Guru cleared another big ignorance of the traditional thinkers. He stated that there was no place called Heaven nor any called Hell where, after death, people will go for eternity. Gurbani explains that living according to the Will of the Lord, keeping Him always in mind and singing His Virtues, is being in Heaven. Hell is suffering from ego, lust, greed, anger, jealousy or slander, etc.

ਤਹਾ ਬੈਕੁੰਠੁ ਜਹ ਕੀਰਤਨੁ ਤੇਰਾ ...... ॥   (Guru Granth, p. 749)

ਨਰਕਿ ਪਰਹਿ ਤੇ ਮਾਨਈ ਜੋ ਹਰਿ ਨਾਮ ਉਦਾਸ ॥

(Guru Granth, p. 1369)

God is our Father; we all are His children, hence equal. No one of us by birth is superior or inferior to others.

ਤੂੰ ਸਾਝਾ ਸਾਹਿਬੁ ਬਾਪੁ ਹਮਾਰਾ ॥   (Guru Granth, p. 97)

112

This makes the Sikh faith unique and fundamentally different from other faiths, wherein it is believed that only followers of their own faith will be saved through their prophet, while rest will be sent to Hell. These radical principles established by Guru Nanak founded for whole humanity a new faith which has been accepted to be the faith of the new age (chapter III).

To preach and practice his mission, Guru Nanak founded the institutions of *Sangat* and *Pangat*. All people participate as equals, without any kind of discrimination on the basis of one's faith, caste, color, or country. They sit together, pray together, and eat together as children of the same Father. They conclude their prayer with a request *"May God bless whole humanity."*

ਤੇਰੇ ਭਾਣੇ ਸਰਬਤ ਦਾ ਭਲਾ ॥   (Sikh Prayer)

NOT A SYNCRETIC FAITH

Against all what has been stated above, some writers still think that Sikhism is a combination of good points taken both from Hinduism and Islam. Some native Sikhs, who have not studied their faith, feel pleased with this observation. Such scholars have observed Nanak from a distance only. They did not care to look into the basics of the faith. Allah of Nanak loves not only Muslims but Hindus and other people as well. Similarly Ram of Nanak loves not just Hindus but the whole humanity. Allah and Ram are two names of the same Lord of Humanity. This concept disproves the above assumption.

Further, both Hinduism and Islam believe in the existence of Heaven and Hell where, after death, human souls will be rewarded or punished according to their faith. Guru Nanak, however, tells that they are mere mythological concepts and not physical places anywhere in the Universe. Sikhs, therefore, are advised not to care for Heaven or Hell. The mission of a Sikh is "Love God and revel in His virtues, always thanking for His blessings."

Religion is known not from the moral code but from the philosophy of the faith regarding the definition of God and the mission of human life prescribed by it. According to the teachings of Nanak, both these concepts are different from those of Islam, Hinduism or any other faith. Sikhism is unique and independent of the religious beliefs of the East and West. It is the faith for the modern man and for all of humanity. This has been observed by many scholars who have studied the faith devotedly and their observations are given in Chapter III.

UNIQUE MIRI-PIRI PRINCIPLE

(A) MIRI-PIRI

'Miri' refers to social and political life while 'Piri' refers to religious beliefs. Guru Nanak preached that the two have a symbiotic relationship and must move hand in hand to serve society effectively. Religion provides the motivation for serving people while political thought creates a social structure for providing actual service to society. In other words, the common objective of the two institutions, religion and politics, is providing service and justice to the people. These two privileges are considered their birth right.

Guru Nanak, however, found that people having political power or religious authority were draining the blood of the weak instead of serving them with honesty and sincerity. The major pillars of the faith, love for the people, commitment for service, and practice of truth were missing from the minds of the men in power. Guru Nanak raised a loud and forceful voice against these antisocial elements.

ਰਾਜੇ ਸੀਹ ਮੁਕਦਮ ਕੁਤੇ ॥   (Guru Granth, p. 1288)

The rulers and their officials behave like blood-sucking beasts.

ਕਾਦੀ ਕੂੜੁ ਬੋਲਿ ਮਲੁ ਖਾਇ ॥ ਬ੍ਰਾਹਮਣੁ ਨਾਵੈ ਜੀਆ ਘਾਇ ॥
ਜੋਗੀ ਜੁਗਤਿ ਨਾ ਜਾਣੈ ਅੰਧੁ ॥ ਤੀਨੇ ਓਜਾੜੇ ਕਾ ਬੰਧੁ ॥

(Guru Granth, p. 662)

The Muslim Kazis (Judges) are corrupt, the Brahmans suck the blood of the innocent, and the Yogis mislead people. They themselves don't know the path for peace and are responsible for the problems of the people (instead of being helpful and sympathetic to them).

The significance of these efforts of Guru Nanak can be properly understood only when one keeps in mind that all kinds of privileges were reserved for only the rulers; the subjects had no rights, not even to express their hurt feelings. Guru Nanak gave new directions to those who wanted to be truly religious persons or political leaders. He preached :

(i) ਰਾਜੇ ਚੁਲੀ ਨਿਆਵ ਕੀ.......॥   (Guru Granth, p. 1240)

114

In his introdu...
of the Sikhs published by UNESCO,
important prophetic observation. He stated :

> *Mankind's religious future may be obscure, yet one thing*
> *can be foreseen. The living higher religions are going to*
> *influence each other more than even before, in the days*
> *of increasing communications between all parts of the*
> *world and branches of the human race. In this coming*
> *religious debate, the Sikh religion and its scriptures, the*
> *Adi Granth, will have something special of value to say*
> *to the rest of the world.*

People in search of peace and truth have already started
shopping around. George W. Cornell in his article, "Gazing into
Religious[1] Future", quoted Leazer, who wrote :

> *If one denomination does not offer a particular item,*
> *people will go to another faith to find it. The megatrend*
> *of pluralism will further swell the shifting of members*
> *among denominations. Already, Gallup poll statistics*
> *show a whopping increase in that phenomenon. For*
> *example, in 1955, only one in 24 Americans left the faith*
> *of childhood to join another denomination, but by 1985,*
> *that migration had grown to one in three—a third of all*
> *members.*[2]

While searching for peace, Pearl S. Buck, a Nobel laureate,
described her experience in the introduction to the translation of
Sri Guru Granth Sahib by Dr. Gopal Singh Dardi :

> *I have studied the scriptures of the great religions, but I*
> *do not find elsewhere the same power of appeal to the*
> *heart and mind as I find here in these volumes... They*
> *speak to a person of any religion or of none. They speak*
> *for the human heart and the searching mind.*

Interfaith discussions are already at the prime of their
popularity. There are innumerable interfaith groups at all levels,

---

1. This topic was included in view of some misunderstanding being
   created regarding the Sikh faith by some writers. This topic repeats
   some of the Sikh philosophies mentioned earlier in the book.
2. Saturday, May 5, 1990, The Free Lance Star, Virginia.

local, national, and international. The World Conference of Religions for Peace (WCRP), recognized by United Nations Organization (UNO), holds its world level conference after every four years. About a decade ago at New Jersey, they observed :

> Too often the names and practices of our religions have been associated with warfare and strife. Now we must reverse this by :
> (i) Breaking down barriers of prejudice and hostility between religious communities and institutions.
> (ii) Confronting the powers of the world with the teachings of our religions rather than conforming to them when they act contrary to the well-being of humanity.
> (iii) Building interreligious understanding in our local communities.

Is this not Sikhism defined in modern terminology ? Does it not mean that the principles laid down for humanity by Guru Nanak five centuries ago, have been accepted by leaders of all the world religions ? Surprisingly, in addition to the philosophy of *Sangat* and *Pangat,* the W.C.R.P. also endorsed the unique *Miri-Piri* concept of the Sikh faith under item (ii) above.

Have not the words of the Rev. H.L. Bradshaw, published a long time back in the Sikh Review, Calcutta, come true? His observations are very clear and emphatic. He stated :

> Sikhism is a Universal World Faith....a message for all men. This is amply illustrated in the writings of the Gurus. Sikhs must cease to think of their faith as just another good religion and must begin to think of Sikhism being the religion for this New Age.

(A) UNITY OF RELIGIONS ?

Some scholars, for their selfish motives have started writings to prove 'unity of religions', that is, all religions are the same. Scholastic jugglery to find quotations from Gurbani and set them against those of other faiths to prove the "Unity of Religions" is a misplaced enthusiasm. By relying on common points, such as remember God, love thy neighbour, help the needy, refrain from violence, do not tell a lie, do not cheat, etc., one cannot prove the unity of religions. All such statements or principles are accepted even by the agnostics as essential for becoming good human beings. If one wants to prove the "unity of religions" by proving that most of the principles are the same in all religions, no research work is needed for that. It can be right away stated that as all religions believe in God, therefore there is unity of religions. However, such statements mislead the people because they conceal a lot.

Constitutions of the two countries may not be the same, just because both punish robbers and reward good workers. One may be a democracy and the other a dictatorship. Similarly, two religions cannot be equated just because both say, "Love thy neighbour. Do not steal." To understand a religion, we must know its definition for God and its mission of human life. Quoting hymns from different religious scriptures to compare their principles is meaningless. While doing so, the writer ignores the basic philosophies of the two faiths compared.

Let us consider an example to understand how comparing quotations and words from two scriptures can mislead the reader. Christians believe that God accepts only Christians and throws all other people into Hell even if they love Him sincerely. According to the Sikh faith, God loves everyone, believers and non-believers alike. Therefore the statement "God loves us" has a different meaning when stated by a Christian and when said by a Sikh. Because of the basic differences among the faiths, comparative statements of their morals may give a totally wrong picture of the faith to the reader.

Christians belive all people are born sinners. To be saved one must have faith in the only begotten Son of God, the Christ, who took upon him all the sins of the people. On the other hand, Gurbani says that all people are born blessed. God grants us this valuable life in order to know and love His virtues.

With these facts before us, believing in the "unity of religions" is showing ignorance of the Sikh faith.

We may go on saying all religions are the same and there is unity of religions, however science has shaken the foundations of the major old faiths. The Pope appeared personally on television on October 5, 1989 to regret the imprisonment given to Galileo about three centuries ago. He agreed that the scientist was right and the Pope, who ordered his punishment, was wrong. The 'crime' of Galileo was his discovery that the earth revolves around the sun, which was against what is mentioned in the Bible.

During the 19th century, Darwin suffered all kinds of abuses from the Christians, just because he suggested the theory of the evolution of man. This challenged the concept of creation in the Bible. This theory, now having been accepted to be largely true, is causing serious concerns for people who believe the Bible to be the word of God.

In general, if confronted with two opposing beliefs one given by science and the other mentioned in religious scriptures, people tend to accept the finding of science.

> *Christianity may well be thriving in parts of Africa and Asia today, but in the West, Christian faith is eroding at an alarming rate. Secular humanism is fast becoming the prevailing "religion" of the Western world. For instance, it is no longer true to describe either Canada or England as a Christian country, since the vast majority of their respective populations have no traditional ties with any religious body. (The Church of England alone has closed nine hundred churches since 1974.) Add to this the fact that only a small fraction of children and young people now receive any religious instruction whatever, and the prognosis for the year 2000 looks very bleak indeed.[1]*

Tom Harper holds science and technology mainly responsible for this erosion. Not just millions but billions of dollars spent on preaching will have no effect on the people unless the message has a value for the scientific man of today. New churches are appearing which do not adhere to the 'old' concepts. The Unitarian and Universalist churches do not accept Christ as the Savior or as the only Son of God.

In India too, people worshipped (some do it even today) the sun, the moon, and other Heavenly bodies as gods. Science has given them a new message.

On the other hand, when we go through Gurbani, we find that it limits itself to the purpose of human life, which is to love God. The best method of doing so, according to Gurbani, is to love people, serve them and "see" God living in them. Gurbani

---

1. Page 4 of *For Christ's Sake*, 1984, by Tom Harper of the Toronto Star.

is a message, not just for Sikhs, but for all people and for all ages.

While laying down its own path for human beings, Gurbani unambiguously and emphatically disagrees with the old beliefs of sectarian faiths.

(i) Because of their ignorance some people worship idols while others worship graves. They waste their life in hollow rituals and fail to realize the truth.

(ii) The Kazis (judges) are corrupt, the Brahmans suck the blood of the innocent, and the Yogis mislead people. They themselves don't know the path for peace and are responsible for the problems of the people.

(iii) This human life has been gifted to us to love people and realize His presence everywhere.

(iv) One Almighty has created this universe and it works under His Will. He alone prevails everywhere, we should sing His virtues to realize Him.

(v) There is no other worship than to love Him.

(vi) I do not believe in Hinduism or Islam. I love the Almighty, the Lord of our bodies and souls, Who is addressed as Ram by Hindus and Allah by Muslims.

(vii) The mission of this human life is to accept His Will and thus realize Him.

(i) ਕੋਊ ਬੁਤਾਨ ਕੋ ਪੂਜਤ ਹੈ ਪਸੁ ਕੋਊ ਮ੍ਰਿਤਾਨ ਕੋ ਪੂਜਨ ਧਾਇਓ ॥
    ਕੂਰ ਕ੍ਰਿਆ ਉਰਝਿਓ ਸਭ ਹੀ ਜਗ ਸ੍ਰੀ ਭਗਵਾਨ ਕੋ ਭੇਦੁ ਨ ਪਾਇਓ ॥
                                                    (Dasam Granth, pp. 14-15)

(ii) ਕਾਦੀ ਕੂੜੁ ਬੋਲਿ ਮਲੁ ਖਾਇ ॥ ਬ੍ਰਾਹਮਣੁ ਨਾਵੈ ਜੀਆ ਘਾਇ ॥
     ਜੋਗੀ ਜੁਗਤਿ ਨ ਜਾਣੈ ਅੰਧੁ ॥ ਤੀਨੇ ਓਜਾੜੇ ਕਾ ਬੰਧੁ ॥
                                                    (Guru Granth, p. 662)

(iii) ਭਈ ਪਰਾਪਤਿ ਮਾਨੁਖ ਦੇਹੁਰੀਆ ॥
      ਗੋਬਿੰਦ ਮਿਲਣ ਕੀ ਇਹ ਤੇਰੀ ਬਰੀਆ ॥   (Guru Granth, p. 12)

(iv) ਏਕੋ ਹੁਕਮੁ ਵਰਤੈ ਸਭ ਲੋਈ ॥ ਏਕਸੁ ਤੇ ਸਭ ਓਪਤਿ ਹੋਈ ॥
     ਰਾਹ ਦੋਵੈ ਖਸਮੁ ਏਕੋ ਜਾਣੁ ॥ ਗੁਰ ਕੈ ਸਬਦਿ ਹੁਕਮੁ ਪਛਾਣੁ ॥
     ਸਗਲ ਰੂਪ ਵਰਨ ਮਨ ਮਾਹੀ ॥ ਕਹੁ ਨਾਨਕ ਏਕੋ ਸਾਲਾਹੀ ॥
                                                    (Guru Granth, p. 223)

(v) ਪੂਜਾ ਕੀਚੈ ਨਾਮੁ ਧਿਆਈਐ ਬਿਨੁ ਨਾਵੈ ਪੂਜ ਨ ਹੋਇ ॥
                                                    (Guru Granth, p. 489)

(vi) ਨਾ ਹਮ ਹਿੰਦੂ ਨ ਮੁਸਲਮਾਨ॥ ਅਲਹ ਰਾਮ ਕੇ ਪਿੰਡੁ ਪਰਾਨ॥

(Guru Granth, p. 1136)

(vii) ਨਾਨਕ ਹੁਕਮੁ ਪਛਾਣਿ ਕੈ ਤਉ ਖਸਮੈ ਮਿਲਣਾ॥

(Guru Granth, p. 139)

Unfortunately, a few Sikh interfaith activists are trying to prove unity of religions and that the "real method of worship" is the same in all religions. They indirectly say that Gurus did not understand the "real worship" of other faiths when they criticized their beliefs and method of worship. These people, thus, give misinformation about the Sikh faith and lower its image while trying to build up their own thesis of the unity of religions. **The Sikh faith when presented without distorting its spirit, meets the needs of all people, whatever their faith. In this sense Sikhism as such is an Interfaith religion.**

(B) NOT RELIGIONS BUT ALL PEOPLE ARE EQUAL

The purpose of interfaith organizations is to develop goodwill for all persons and understand their beliefs. The Sikh faith is built on the foundation of loving all people irrespective of their faith, appearance, language, or culture. Sikhs, therefore, don't need another "Interfaith" for developing understanding among people of different religions.

These principles and the position of the Sikh faith must be explained to the members of all other faiths. The fact that Sikhs believe in ONE God and in the brotherhood of humanity must be pointed out emphatically. Just because there are limitless names for God (Allah, Ram, Gobind, Guru, God, etc.) does not mean there are many faiths or religions.

Another equally incorrect statement is made by scholars who know the Sikh faith from a distance only. They say that Sikhism is a combination of good points from Hinduism and Islam. Such misleading statements conceal the fact that Sikhism is a sovereign faith revealed by Guru Nanak. It has nothing to do with the beliefs of old faiths including Hinduism, Islam, and Yoga.

The truth revealed by Guru Nanak should not be distorted to fit ones' thoughts to make him a multi-faith activist. The Sikh faith, as mentioned earlier, respects all people whatever their faith but diagrees with the philosophy and methods of worship of

122

other faiths. In the interfaith meetings, one should not hesitate to speak this truth even though it may be contrary to the faith of the listeners. The World Conference of Religions for Peace and other philosophers as quoted above have frankly agreed to the universalities of the basic Sikh principles. The Sikh participants in the interfaith functions may refer to their opinions as well.

In the end, it must be emphasized that the principles of the Sikh faith must not be twisted to fit it into the present day thoughts of the pseudo leaders of the faith.

CHAPTER IX

CONCLUDING OVERVIEW

UNIVERSAL MESSAGE

Guru Nanak gave a universal message : *Do not divide people into different faiths or castes. Love for all people without discrimination is the highest religion.* For preaching this, he founded the institutions of *Sangat* and *Pangat,* where all people sing together the praises of the Father-Mother, the Creator and eat together as equals.

He observed that religion, instead of helping the community, was harming people because of false concepts preached to the people. Rather than creating love and affection, it was spreading hatred among them. Human beings were split into upper castes and lower castes. Some people were considered even untouchable, their touch was considered to desecrate a temple or defile an upper class Hindu.

The Guru protested strongly against such beliefs. He declared that it was a sin to regard any individual as an untouchable, just because that person was born to a so-called low caste mother. He said those people, who commit the sin of hating or harassing other human beings, because of their birth or caste, are themselves 'low caste'. On the other hand those persons, who consider all people as one brotherhood, belong to the 'highest caste'.

ਆਈ ਪੰਥੀ ਸਗਲ ਜਮਾਤੀ ਮਨਿ ਜੀਤੈ ਜਗੁ ਜੀਤੁ ॥

(Guru Granth, P. 6)

He preached that every human being has been created by God. Therefore, all people are equal; no one is inferior or superior by birth. In His court, we are judged by our deeds and not by our birth.

Secondly, the rulers were tyrannical and unjust. They would commit any kind of crime against non-Muslims to gain popularity with their fellow Muslim leaders. The support of Muslim priests, they thought, was necessary for them to remain in power. Therefore, not only were non-Muslims denied equal human rights,

but demoralizing, torturing, or even killing them was considered a religious act. Hindus expressed their hatred for Muslims by calling them *Malechh,* or dirty foreign people.

Men having political, social, or economic power were sucking the blood of the common people by whatever method they could. Guru Nanak raised his voice against such tyrants to protect the human rights of the weak. The Guru compared unjust and cruel kings with blood sucking beasts. The corrupt and greedy officials were described as the nails (tools) of these 'beasts'.

ਰਾਜੇ ਸੀਹ ਮੁਕਦਮ ਕੁਤੇ ॥ ਜਾਇ ਜਗਾਇਨਿ ਬੈਠੇ ਸੁਤੇ ॥
ਚਾਕਰ ਨਹਦਾ ਪਾਇਨਿ ਘਾਉ ॥ ਰਤੁ ਪਿਤੁ ਕੁਤਿਹੋ ਚਟਿ ਜਾਹੁ ॥

(Guru Granth, p. 1288)

Thirdly, women were considered second grade citizens and non-pious human beings. Woman was supposed to have been created to serve and please man. In Hindu society, after the death of a person, last rites could be performed only by a son or brother and not by a daughter or sister of the deceased. Women were not permitted to participate in many religious activities.

Guru Nanak fought against all these evils and founded the institutions of *Sangat* and *Pangat* in which all persons irrespective of their faith, birth, sex, color, or country were treated as equals. This was practiced and preached by the nine Gurus succeeding him and by the Khalsa Panth, the corporate body of the Sikhs. Mutual hatred for different religions and castes was replaced by love for all humanity.

To motivate people to live a virtuous life, Guru Nanak emphatically denied that he or any other prophet could save or help any person at the time of *final* judgement. During his visit to the Mecca Sharif, when asked who are superior, Hindus or Muslims, Nanak replied, "Without good deeds, both will repent." Sikhism thus brought a social and religious revolution.

SIKH CHARACTER

After the death of Guru Gobind Singh, the Sikhs had to manage their own affairs through the *Panj Pyara* institution. Under the guidance of Banda Bahadur they conquered about half of Panjab. After the murder of Banda, the Sikhs suffered inhuman persecutions, continuous harassment, and massacre. The more violent the methods adopted to suppress the Sikhs, the more firm

125

in their faith the Sikhs became. For many years, just being a Sikh was a crime punishable by death. Sikhs gave up their homes and started to live mostly in forests, hills, and other inaccessible places. During all these trying times, they stuck to their ideal character. This period is called the Golden Period of the Sikh nation. Some repetition of the description of their character will not be out of place here.

When Banda attacked Sirhind to kill the oppressive governor, he did not touch Sirhind Sharif, the religious place of the Muslims. Here is buried Mujaddid Alaf Saani, the Muslim priest, who plotted the execution of Guru Arjun Dev. This behavior was in total contrast to what was later done to the Harimandar Sahib, Amritsar by the rulers and the invading Muslims.

The Sikhs defeated and took over all Muslims rulers between the rivers of Jamuna and Ravi but not the Nawab of Malerkotla. The Nawab was protected because he had pleaded for the human rights of the two younger sons of Guru Gobind Singh. He had told the governor, "These children are innocent. It is a crime to kill them." Thus the uprising of the Panjabis led by the Sikhs was not against Muslims or Islam but it was against the tyranny of the rulers. The death statement of Banda Singh supports this.

> When a Mughal nobleman said to Banda, "It is surprising that one, who shows so much acuteness in his features and so much nobility in his conduct, should have been guilty of such horrors." Banda replied, "I will tell you. Whenever men become corrupt and wicked as to relinquish the path of equity and abandon themselves to all kinds of excesses, then providence never fails to raise up a scourage like me to chastise a race so depraved; but when the measure of punishment is full, then he raises up men like you to bring him to punishment."

(*The History of the Sikhs*, Khushwant Singh, p. 117)

THE GOAL ACHIEVED :
CHANGE IN HUMAN HEARTS

The Sikhs were finally strong enough to take over Lahore in 1765 and rule Panjab. They showed due regard to all citizens. No resident of the city had his possessions looted nor was any body ill-treated. A few months occupation of the city by the Khalsa removed the anti-Sikh feelings created by the Afghans,

Mughals and Muslim priests for their own narrow political advantage. Fear of the Khalsa was gone from the Muslim mind. Sikhs were treated as fellow Panjabis rather than anti-Muslims or *Kafirs*. On the other hand, Afghans were considered as foreigners rather than as saviors of the faith as they had projected themselves all the time. Sikhs were no longer feared as robbers but depended upon as freedom fighters desiring to restore human rights.

These opinions regarding Sikhs were very strong among the Muslims, when Ahmed Shah reoccupied Lahore in 1766. Therefore, they advised him to offer the governorship of Panjab to Sikhs in his own best interest and that of the citizens. Ahmed accepted the advice and invited the leader of the Sikhs to govern Panjab by sending a special tray of high quality dry fruit from his country. Lehna Singh, the leader of the Khalsa, politely declined the offer by telling the envoy that fruit sent by Ahmed were meant for royalties only, and that he was a mere peasant who liked simple food. The actual reason for this non-acceptance was evident to everyone. All knew that the Panjabi people were not going to be ruled any longer by force from Delhi or from Kabul but were strong enough to take care of themselves. Lehna Singh wondered in his mind why he should accept the offer to rule Panjab from a foreign invader when the people themselves were willing to welcome Sikh rule.

After looting the people, Ahmed left for Kabul; the governor of Lahore knew well that he could not count on the cooperation of even the Muslim residents. The leading Muslim citizens frankly told him that they were happy with the Sikhs and would welcome them by opening the doors of the city to them at night. They advised the governor that instead of being held as a prisoner or being killed by Sikhs, he should settle with them for a pension for himself and hand over the rule of Lahore to the Sikhs.

Not only their persistent resistance to state terrorism, but also their character and their behaviour as protectors of human rights and welfare of the common man, were responsible for making Sikhs the rulers of Panjab. Historians have noted that it was for the first time in the history of the state, that the Raj (rule) of Ranjit Singh was a government of the people, by the people, and for the people. All communities, Hindus, Muslims, and Sikhs,

127

enjoyed equal rights, both as rulers and as citizens. Not a single person was given a death sentence by the Maharaja during his long rule for four decades.

APPEAL TO THE YOUTH

Before closing this last chapter of the book, the author appeals to the youth to enjoy the benefits of the philosophy of Guru Nanak so ideally suited for modern times. Let them keep in mind the high ideals of life laid down by the Gurus and practiced both in letter and spirit by the Sikhs of the 18th century. During the British rule, the high Sikh character and their firm belief in sacrificing everything for human rights were recently observed by the whole world. It is the ideal Sikh character, which is going to make young people better individuals or Sikhs. Once this movement becomes popular with the Sikh youth, people will love them and respect the Sikh faith and its followers. They will be considered the saviors of the misguided youth in the same way as the Sikhs in Panjab were considered the protectors of human rights two centuries ago.

The Sikh youth can enjoy self-esteem and develop self-confidence by owning their glorious heritage. The golden future is before them, if they sincerely believe in, understand and practice the Sikh philosophy. **Unless the Sikh character is practiced by the youth in their daily life, how can non-Sikhs know that it is great to be a Sikh? If young people owing their allegiance to Sikh faith are addicted to drugs, alcohol, bad habits, and antisocial behavior as other youth are, how can they communicate to the people that Sikh faith and high character go together?** We have to tread the path laid down for us by the Gurus and not allow ourselves to be derailed by the pressures of modern society. The firm decision of the mind that the right path has to be stuck to whatever the circumstances helps everyone greatly. It brings real peace and bliss which most of us wish to enjoy.